Controlling the Frontier

Southern Africa 1806-1828, the Cape Frontier Wars and the Fetcani Alarm

Hugh Driver

Helion & Company

Helion & Company Limited
Unit 8 Amherst Business Centre
Budbrooke Road
Warwick
CV34 5WE
England
Tel. 01926 499 619
Email: info@helion.co.uk
Website: www.helion.co.uk
Twitter: @helionbooks
Visit our blog at blog.helion.co.uk

Published by Helion & Company 2023
Designed and typeset by Mach 3 Solutions (www.mach3solutions.co.uk)
Cover designed by Paul Hewitt, Battlefield Design (www.battlefield-design.co.uk)

Text © Hugh Driver 2023
Images © as individually assigned
Maps drawn by George Anderson © Helion & Company 2023

Cover: Meeting between Batavian Governor General J.W. Janssens and Xhosa chief Ngqika at the Kat River, 1803 (Aquatint published in Amsterdam in 1810 by Evert Maaskamp, from drawing by Paravicini di Capelli)

Every reasonable effort has been made to trace copyright holders and to obtain their permission for the use of copyright material. The author and publisher apologize for any errors or omissions in this work, and would be grateful if notified of any corrections that should be incorporated in future reprints or editions of this book.

ISBN 978-1-915113-78-8

British Library Cataloguing-in-Publication Data.
A catalogue record for this book is available from the British Library.

All rights reserved. No part of this publication may be reproduced, stored in a retrieval system, or transmitted, in any form, or by any means, electronic, mechanical, photocopying, recording or otherwise, without the express written consent of Helion & Company Limited.

For details of other military history titles published by Helion & Company Limited contact the above address or visit our website: http://www.helion.co.uk.

We always welcome receiving book proposals from prospective authors.

In Memoriam
Smeda Mazyanga Kaira Gondwe
Born 25 December 1939
Died 21 July 2021
Mother-in-Law to the author, mother to Wilson, Charity, John, and Betty, and foster mother to the orphaned of Chingola. She saw past all races and tribes to leave the world a better place:
'Well done, good and faithful servant …'
Matthew 25:23

Contents

List of Illustrations	vi
List of Maps	ix
Acknowledgements	x
Author's Note	xi
1 Background: The Eastern Frontier	13
2 The Fifth Cape Frontier War	38
3 Colonial Forces Beyond the Frontier: The Fetcani Alarm	87
Bibliography	124
Index	128

List of Illustrations

'Boors Returning from Hunting', aquatint published November 1804 by the artist and traveller Samuel Daniell, 1775-1811. (*African Scenery and Animals at the Cape of Good Hope*: 'elephant folio' containing thirty coloured aquatints, published in parts, Cleveland Street, Fitzroy Square, London, 1804-05)   14

Ngqika c.1775-1829, chief of the Rharhabe or western Xhosa. Watercolour from manuscript journal of Willem Bartholomeus Eduard Paravicini di Capelli, 1778-1848, onetime officer of the 'Corps of Free Hottentots'. (*Reize In de Binnen-Landen van Zuid-Africa. Gedaan in den Jaare 1803 door W.B.E. Paravicini di Capelli, Kapitein Aide de Camp, by de Gouverneur van de Caap de Goede Hoop*: subsequently published by the Van Riebeeck Society, ed. W.J. de Kock, Cape Town, 1965)   15

John Graham when a lieutenant in the 90th Foot, from which he transferred to the 93rd (as reproduced by Cory, *Rise of South Africa* 1, 1910, from painting 'in possession of F.C.G. Graham, Esq. ... of Grahamstown')   16

Colonel Graham's projected uniform for the Cape Regiment, 1810. (National Archives, London)   16

Young Boer huntsman, from a sketch by Samuel Daniell. (Museum Africa, previously Africana Museum)   18

Xhosa hunting elephant along the Great Fish River (as reproduced by Cory, *Rise of South Africa* 1, 1910, from painting 'in possession of Rev. Dr. Flint, of Cape Town')   20

Hottentot (Khoikhoi) soldier, Cape Regiment. (Museum Africa, previously Africana Museum)   21

Portrait of a Xhosa chief, ascribed to a dragoon officer in the force under Graham's command. (*A Collection of Portraits of the Savage Tribes inhabiting the Boundaries of the Colony of the Cape of Good Hope. Taken from Life in 1812, by an Officer of the 21st Lt. Dragoons, engaged in an Expedition against those Tribes, under Lt. Col. Graham*, McQueen & Co., lithograph, published by Edwd. Orme, Bond St, London, 1822)   22

LIST OF ILLUSTRATIONS

Clearing the bush, from a lithograph by the Grahamstown artist Frederick Timpson I'Ons. (I'Ons was a volunteer in the Sixth Frontier War of 1834-35) — 24

Thomas Pringle (1789-1834): 1820 Settler, journalist, poet, humanitarian and Whig leaning activist. (Stipple and line engraving by William Finden, published by Edward Moxon, Dover Street, London, 1837) — 25

Hottentot (Khoikhoi) bugle boy, Cape Regiment, sketched by ensign R.H. Dingley, October 1816. (Museum Africa, previously Africana Museum) — 27

Plan of Grahamstown in 1814. (Cory, *Rise of South Africa* 1) — 29

An example of the earliest properties built with the establishment of Grahamstown. (Cory, *Rise of South Africa* 1, from painting 'in possession of Rev. Dr. Flint, of Cape Town') — 30

Earliest known picture of Grahamstown, reputedly painted by Thomas Philipps's wife, Charlotte, and thus after the arrival of the 1820 Settlers. The house of future Voortrekker leader Piet Retief is indicated centre right; the fighting in 1819 took place over the undulating ground to the left. (Albany Museum) — 35

Lord Charles Somerset, 1767-1831: Governor of the Cape, 1814-1826. (Pen and pencil sketch, National Library of South Africa, Cape Town) — 36

Meeting between Batavian military governor, J.W. Janssens, and Xhosa chief, Ngqika, at the Kat River in 1803. Lord Charles Somerset met the Xhosa chiefs Ngqika and Ndlambe in similar fashion in April 1817. (Aquatint published in Amsterdam in 1810 by Evert Maaskamp, from drawing by Paravicini di Capelli. Issued as an accompaniment to *De Kaffers aan de Zuidkust van Afrika* by former landdrost of Uitenhage and early European authority on the Xhosa, Johann Christoph Ludwig [Lodewijk] Alberti, 1768-1812) — 37

Debe Nek, with Ntaba kaNdoda looming in the background. Site of the Battle of Amalinde, October 1818. (Cory, *Rise of South Africa* 1, 1910) — 47

WMS missionary, William James Shrewsbury, whose journal and letters constitute an important source both for the Battle of Amalinde and the 'Fetcani alarm'. — 48

Andries Stockenström, 1792-1864, a portrait taken in middle age and subsequently used as the frontispiece of his autobiography — 52

'The Steerage of a Transport' on the Cape run: sketch by ensign R.H. Dingley, Cape Regiment. (Museum Africa, previously Africana Museum) — 54

Cavalry of the Cape Corps. (Museum Africa, previously Africana Museum) — 56

The Fish River, onetime eastern boundary of the Cape Colony — 59

Grahamstown: watercolour attributed to 'an officer' after the Fifth Frontier War, Graham's tree still visible centre left, and post-war Drostdy House far right. Cory reproduced these images and dated them 1824. Certainly there is no church, which was begun that year. The drostdy was left unfinished in 1823, being one of Retief's unfulfilled contracts, precipitating his bankruptcy. — 62

Spruit on the eastern side of Grahamstown, with barracks to the left, scene of the fiercest fighting in 1819. (Cory, *Rise of South Africa* 1, 1910)	63
Xhosa warrior, lithograph, frontispiece from T.J. Lucas, *Pen and Pencil Reminiscences of a Campaign in South Africa* (London: Day & Son, 1861). Note bundle of assegais and kaross, both carried in left hand.	65
Boer commando, a sketch by coppersmith, engraver and pioneer Cape photographer, William Syme, 1824-1866. (Museum Africa, previously Africana Museum)	71
Trompetter's Drift with Fish River in flood. (Cory, *Rise of South Africa* II, 1913)	72
A subsequent depiction of close quarters bush fighting on the eastern frontier, by artist and explorer Thomas Baines, 1820-1875. (Museum Africa, previously Africana Museum)	75
Xhosa village, aquatint published by Evert Maaskamp, from album *Description physique et historique des Cafres, sur la cote meridionale de l'Afrique*, Amsterdam 1811 (but originally issued as an accompaniment to *De Kaffers aan de Zuidkust van Afrika*, Amsterdam 1810), by Lodewijk Alberti.	77
British forces crossing the Kei, painting by Thomas Baines. (Museum Africa, previously Africana Museum)	77
Colonel Christopher Chapman Bird (1769-1861): Colonial Secretary, Cape Colony, 1818-1824. (Cory, *Rise of South Africa* II, 1913)	78
Hintsa (c.1790-1835), chief of the amaGcaleka and paramount chief of the Xhosa. (Frontispiece from *Narrative of a Voyage of Observation among the Colonies of Western Africa … and of a Campaign in Kaffir-Land on the Staff of the Commander-in-Chief in 1835*, Vol. I, by James Edward Alexander [London: Henry Colburn, 1837], with maps and plates by Major Charles Collier Michell, 1793-1851: Surveyor General and Civil Engineer, Cape of Good Hope, 1828; Assistant Quartermaster General, Sixth Frontier War, 1834-35)	81
Fort Willshire, from a lithograph (erroneously labelled 'Caffer Fair Fort Wiltshire') in Andrew Steedman, *Wanderings and Adventures in the Interior of Southern Africa* (London: Longman & Co., 1835)	81
Lord Charles Somerset as a captain/lieutenant colonel of the Coldstream Guards (a captaincy in the Guards was equivalent to a lieutenant-colonelcy in another regiment), by the leading portrait painter of the Regency period, Richard Cosway, RA (1742-1821)	85
Lieutenant General Sir Rufane Shaw Donkin (1772-1841), Acting Governor, Cape Colony, January 1820 to November 1821. (Stipple engraving of 1831 executed by 'W. Holl' – William Holl, father or son – from a painting by Henry Mayer, c.1782-1847)	85
'Canteen scene during the frontier wars', oil painting by F.T. I'Ons, of which at least two full copies were made by the Cape Town artist W.H.F.L. Langschmidt (1805-1866). (Fehr Collection, Castle of Good Hope)	86
A sergeant of The Cape Mounted Rifles, depicted by Thomas Baines. (Museum Africa, previously Africana Museum)	89

LIST OF ILLUSTRATIONS

Lieutenant Colonel (later General Sir) Henry Somerset, 1794-1862, eldest son of Lord Charles Somerset and first commanding officer, Cape Mounted Rifles. (19th century lithograph, artist unknown: National Library of South Africa, Cape Town)	89
General Sir Richard Bourke 1777-1855, Acting Governor of the Cape 1826-1828. (1829 lithograph, artist unknown)	94
Thomas Philipps, influential and agitating 1820 Settler, who blamed Vusani (Ngubengcuka) for manipulating Major Dundas into the 'slaughter' of 'innocent individuals' on the Umtata. (Provenance unknown: reproduced as 'privately owned' in H.E. Hockly, *The Story of the British Settlers of 1820 in South Africa*, Cape Town: Juta & Co., 1948)	104
The fort aside, this detail from a contemporary *Illustrated London News* depiction of Xhosa removing their wounded and cattle from (in this case) Trompetter's Drift, provides a good indication of the scene that must have presented itself to Dundas as the Thembu withdrew in the wake of the confused Umtata engagement of 26 July 1828.	105
No illustrations survive of the Battle of Mbholompo, but the manner of fighting experienced is well captured in this later depiction of 'A skirmish in the Open' during the 1850-53 Frontier War. (Lithograph from Lucas, *Pen and Pencil Reminiscences of a Campaign in South Africa*)	112
WMS missionary, Stephen Kay, who denounced the events at Mbholompo. (National Library of South Africa, Cape Town)	116
WMS missionary, William Boyce, who supported the intervention. (National Library of South Africa, Cape Town)	117
Grahamstown, as Private George Witcherley of the 55th Foot would have known it in 1828. The first church was completed in 1830. (Cory, *Rise of South Africa* II, 'from a water-colour sketch by Dr. W.G. Atherstone, 1833, redrawn by F.W. Armstrong, Esq.')	119

List of Maps

The Cape eastern frontier at the time of the Fourth and Fifth Frontier Wars, 1811–1812 and 1818–1819	xii
The Thembu and Mpondo kingdoms c. 1820s	98
'Fetcani' raids 1825–1828	100

Acknowledgements

I should like to make particular mention of the following, without whom I would have struggled to bring this volume to fruition: author, veteran, and experienced editor, Chris Cocks, who has been a good friend for what must now be a decade, and who is always my first port of call when issues of a technical nature arise (and who has never failed to respond, at any hour of the day); Ed Hood, Special Collections Archivist at the School of Oriental & African Studies, University of London, who during the period of the COVID pandemic was very kind in ensuring that I received scans of the Shrewsbury correspondence; the staff of the Templer Study Centre, National Army Museum, London; Dr Christopher Brice, *From Musket to Maxim, 1815–1914* series editor, who demonstrated exemplary professionalism and patience throughout the whole process of production, but not least when suggesting discriminating improvements and clarifications to the text; George Anderson, cartographer for the series, who not only produced such clear and accessible maps, but also was a pleasure to work with; and finally Duncan Rogers, Managing Director of Helion, who agreed to publish the book. Thank you all at Helion, named and unnamed.

Hugh Driver
Salperton, Gloucestershire
April 2023

Author's Note

As with all historical studies of the Cape Frontier Wars, some of the language, nomenclature, and views expressed by persons quoted in this book are by their nature likely to be offensive to modern readers. No offense is intended: they will be found, as a matter of historical integrity, only in quotations from contemporary sources and are indicated as such. Throughout the main text demoded usages are not employed.

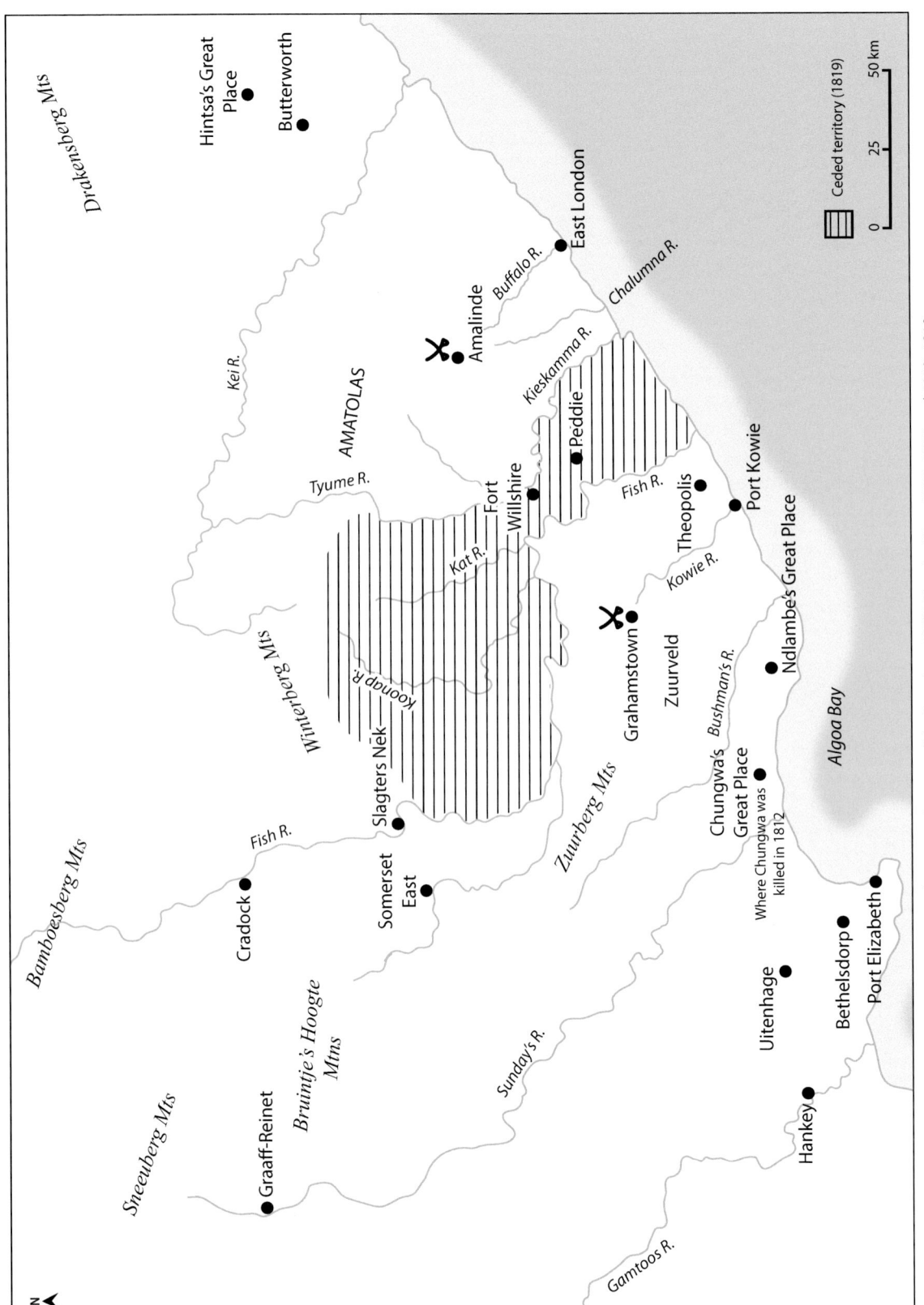

The Cape eastern frontier at the time of the Fourth and Fifth Frontier Wars, 1811–1812 and 1818–1819.

1

Background: The Eastern Frontier

The frontier semi-nomadic Dutch-speaking sheep and cattle farmers of the eighteenth century, known as *Trekboers*, although largely self-sufficient, nevertheless maintained irregular contact with Cape markets and the Cape colonial administration and for the most part saw themselves as Cape subjects. However, as they moved further away from the settled regions of the Cape in search of grazing, and as the Dutch East India Company extended the boundaries of the Cape in an effort to maintain its jurisdiction, so these ties grew weaker and more irksome to them.

From the 1770s the movement eastwards had come into conflict with the Xhosa in the 'sour veld' (*Zuurveld*), west of the Great Fish River. The Xhosa regarded land as communal, by contrast to the Boers, who held property on an individual basis. That is to say, the Xhosa adhered to the communal occupation of grazing lands by specific groupings. They were not nomadic in the manner of the San or Bushmen of the interior. By 1795 the frontier had advanced to the Orange River in the north and the Great Fish River to the east, but the frontier district of Graaff-Reinet was in open rebellion. By that time, after nearly a century and a half of weak Dutch East India Company rule, the inland Cape Dutch had evolved into an isolated, individualistic people, who defined themselves against the black non-Christian populations, whom they characterised as *kaffirs* – the term having its etymological roots in the Arabic word *kafir*, meaning 'unbeliever' or more generally 'one without religion', but incorporating in this case racial superiority and black subservience.

The second British occupation (the first was from 1795 to 1803, followed by a brief period of rule by the Batavian regime then in power in the Netherlands) extended from 1806 to 1814.[1] The Cape was then ceded to Great Britain, becoming a crown colony under the administration of the British

---

[1] The Peace of Amiens was signed in March 1802, but its terms did not go undisputed in Great Britain and the handover of the Cape to the Batavian Republic was officially postponed. It only finally occurred on 21 February 1803: W. Steenkamp, *Assegais, Drums and Dragoons: A Military and Social History of the Cape 1510–1806* (Johannesburg & Cape Town: Jonathan Ball, 2012), pp.174–178.

'Boors Returning from Hunting', aquatint published November 1804 by the artist and traveller Samuel Daniell, 1775–1811. (*African Scenery and Animals at the Cape of Good Hope*: 'elephant folio' containing thirty coloured aquatints, published in parts, Cleveland Street, Fitzroy Square, London, 1804-05)

government. The paramount purpose of its acquisition was to safeguard trade with India, and viewed from that strategic perspective there was little interest in the Cape interior – added to which the need to economise in the wake of the Napoleonic wars impacted on the maintenance of frontier garrisons. The aim was for a fixed, settled frontier, and the Fourth Xhosa or Cape Frontier War of 1811–1812, the first endured during this period of British rule, saw a mixed force under Colonel John Graham drive the Xhosa, led by Ndlambe, back beyond the Fish River with this purpose.

Hintsa (c.1790-1835) was theoretically in line to become paramount chief of the entire Xhosa nation; however, during the rule of Hintsa's grandfather, Gcaleka, the western Xhosa had broken away under Hintsa's great-uncle, Rarabe. Rarabe's son, Mlawu, then died young, so that when Rarabe himself died in about 1787, it was his grandson, Ngqika, who became chief of the ama-Rarabe or Rharhabe, with Mlawu's brother, Ndlambe, acting as Ngqika's guardian and regent of the ama-Rharhabe.

Not content with this, Ndlambe manoeuvred to gain the chieftaincy of the ama-Rharhabe, which led to much animosity – greatly exacerbated when Ngqika took to his side his uncle's concubine, Thuthula. Seen as incest, there was an extensive defection to Ndlambe (whom Ngqika had attempted to keep as a prisoner), and in February 1799 Ndlambe broke away from Ngqika's Great Place and began to establish himself beyond the Great Fish

BACKGROUND: THE EASTERN FRONTIER

River, in the Zuurveld. To this internecine rivalry can be traced much of the unrest developing on the eastern frontier of the colony. That successive Cape governments treated with Ngqika as if he were in fact the paramount chief of the Xhosa nation, investing him with an authority that he was unable to maintain, only added to the difficulties.

However, the complexities of the territorial question and the internal stresses of Xhosa dynastic culture were of little direct concern to Graham at that stage. There was an awareness of the feuding between Ngqika, chief of the western Xhosa, and Ndlambe, his uncle; but Graham believed Ngqika to be 'faithless and treacherous with all the rest' and 'as deeply concerned in the general system of plunder as any other of the Kaffir chiefs', and certainly there was a record of perceived duplicity in recent years.[2]

Development and deployment of the Cape Regiment

The first Cape Coloured unit to be formed by the Dutch East India Company was the 'Corps of Bastard Hottentots' (*Corps Bastaard Hottentots*) in 1781, the other ranks comprising men of mixed Khoikhoi and white ancestry (sometimes called Eurafrican). Reformed as the 'Pandour Corps' (*Corps van Pandoeren*) in 1793, the unit served against the British during the first invasion of the Cape in 1795. During the subsequent first British occupation, the men were then reformed under the British colonial administration as the Cape Corps, before being transferred in 1802 to the Batavian Republic and reformed in 1803 as the 'Corps of Free Hottentots' (*Corps Vrye Hottentotten*) and later 'Hottentot Light Infantry' (*Hottentot Ligte Infanterie*). Its strength at that time was from 500 to 600, with a uniform of blue jacket with red facings, white buttons, and a round hat.[3]

The *Hottentot Ligte Infanterie* performed credibly at the Battle of Blaauwberg in January 1806, and Major General Sir David Baird re-adopted it as the Cape Regiment (although, unofficially, it was still known as the Cape Corps) for service in the colony. The regiment comprised 10 companies, with British officers and Cape Coloured other ranks. Essentially a light infantry corps financed from the colony's funds, it was raised by the then Major

Ngqika c.1775-1829, chief of the Rharhabe or western Xhosa. Watercolour from manuscript journal of Willem Bartholomeus Eduard Paravicini di Capelli, 1778-1848, onetime officer of the 'Corps of Free Hottentots'. (*Reize In de Binnen-Landen van Zuid-Africa. Gedaan in den Jaare 1803 door W.B.E. Paravicini di Capelli, Kapitein Aide de Camp, by de Gouverneur van de Caap de Goede Hoop*: subsequently published by the Van Riebeeck Society, ed. W.J. de Kock, Cape Town, 1965)

---

2 B. Maclennan, *A Proper Degree of Terror: John Graham and the Cape's Eastern Frontier* (Johannesburg: Ravan Press, 1986), pp.89–90.
3 Major G. Tylden, *The Armed Forces of South Africa* (Johannesburg: Trophy Press, 1982), p.49; Steenkamp, *Assegais, Drums and Dragoons*, pp.306–324.

CONTROLLING THE FRONTIER

John Graham when a lieutenant in the 90th Foot, from which he transferred to the 93rd (as reproduced by Cory, *Rise of South Africa* 1, 1910, from painting 'in possession of F.C.G. Graham, Esq. … of Grahamstown')

Colonel Graham's projected uniform for the Cape Regiment, 1810. (National Archives, London)

John Graham of the 93rd Regiment, who was thereupon appointed its local commander with the rank of lieutenant colonel.

Characterised as a 'Hottentot' (Khoikhoi) unit, the rank and file were in fact of mixed racial origin, and to underline its light infantry role the initial grey uniform was presently replaced with the familiar green jacket with black facings. It was the advent of the Fourth Cape Frontier War that saw the Cape Regiment move from its initial headquarters at Wynberg, near Cape Town, to the Eastern Cape.[4]

Fourth Cape Frontier War

As early as 1810 a reluctant Earl of Caledon, Governor of the Cape of Good Hope, had sent 56 officers and men of the 21st Light Dragoons and 105 of the 93rd Foot to the eastern frontier, together with 419 members of the Cape Regiment in their new green uniforms, but there was no decrease in tensions.[5]

---

4 J. de Villiers, *Die Cape Regiment, 1806–1817, 'n Koloniale Regiment in Britse Diens* (Pretoria: Archives Year Book, Die Staatsdrukker, 1989), p.238; Tylden, *Armed Forces of South Africa*, p.57.
5 Maclennan, *Proper Degree of Terror*, pp.65–66.

Caledon's successor, Sir John Cradock, was the first governor to hold both supreme civil and military authority (military governorships subsequently being the norm, until the appointment of Sir George Grey in 1854). Arriving at Cape Town in September 1811, he was immediately confronted with the continuing unrest on the eastern frontier and saw no benefit in equivocation. The task, as he saw it, was one of dealing with those Xhosa who had crossed into the colony and thereafter refused to withdraw across the Great Fish River. So he instructed the magistrates (*landdroste*) of the eastern districts to call up their burghers and placed Lieutenant Colonel John Graham in command of a mixed force with orders to impel the Xhosa to cross back over the border. Graham, who was on the point of leaving the Cape, professed himself astonished to have received the command, but had 'long been of opinion' that it had become necessary to take 'coercive measures against the Caffers'.[6]

On 8 October 1811 Graham boarded the *Upton Castle* – built for trading in the Far East, but which had led an eventful life in the Napoleonic wars, most recently as a transport ship during the invasion of the Isle de France (Mauritius) at the close of 1810. With Graham went 54 men of the 21st Light Dragoons, 48 men of the Royal Artillery (with drivers and guns), 112 men of the 83rd Foot, 246 men of the Cape Regiment and 96 horses. Already stationed on the frontier at that time were 226 British troops and 185 men of the Cape Regiment.

Deployed to the Cape in 1806, the 21st Light Dragoons were to have a brief existence (in this incarnation), having been re-raised in 1794 and selected for disbandment in 1820. However, in that time they played an important role in the Cape Colony, and in 1813 it was to the 21st Dragoons that Captain Abraham Josias Cloete transferred, becoming ADC to the new governor, Lord Charles Somerset, the following year. (In 1842, it was this Cloete who commanded the British force at Port Natal.) To maintain communications between Cape Town and the frontier a system of express riders was established, involving relays of dragoons. By this method the distance could be covered in six days.

The force at Graham's disposal, as it was officially listed with separate officer and subaltern designations, comprised: Royal Artillery, 98 (one officer, 97 rank and file); 21st Dragoons, 165 (seven officers, 11 subalterns, 147 rank and file); Cape Regiment, 594 (30 officers, 42 subalterns, 522 rank and file); 83rd Foot, 221 (eight officers, 13 subalterns, 200 rank and file) and 93rd Foot, three (one officer, one subaltern, one rank and file).[7] But notwithstanding, Cradock directed that Graham should as far as possible use the Boer commandos for the task in hand, 'as the future tranquillity of

---

6 DSAB II, pp.148–149. John Graham to Robert Graham, 12th of Fintry, 4 Oct. 1811: C.T. Atkinson (ed.), *Supplementary Report on the Manuscripts of Robert Graham Esq. of Fintry* (London: HMSO, 1940), pp.82–83.

7 'State of the Troops employed in the Interior, 18 Oct. 1811', cited in J. de Villiers, 'Perspective on John Graham and the Fourth Cape Eastern Frontier War', *New Contree*, No. 68 (December 2013), pp.37–38. Maclennan, *Proper Degree of Terror*, p.89, provides alternative figures: 167 men of the 21st Light Dragoons, 49 men of the Royal Artillery, 221 of the 83rd Foot, three of the 93rd Foot and 431 men of the Cape Regiment. Among them they had 194 horses.

CONTROLLING THE FRONTIER

Young Boer huntsman, from a sketch by Samuel Daniell. (Museum Africa, previously Africana Museum)

the country must be left to their exertions'. That being the case '[i]t would', he thought, 'be unwise to teach them to think that they were not equal to the defence'.[8] Graham therefore in the first instance manned the posts strung out from Algoa Bay with regular troops, intending to initiate the expulsions primarily with the burgher commandos.

It was not a prospect Graham welcomed. Echoing the sentiments given prominence at the turn of the century by John Barrow, Graham later admitted that he saw the frontier Boers as 'the most ignorant of all peasants', lacking discipline and harbouring a 'known antipathy to Hottentots' – meaning the men of the Cape Regiment ('my own lads', as he called them, whom he described as 'certainly the fittest men for the service').[9] There should have been some 500 Boers divided into groups of 50, each under a commandant maintaining authority over two field-cornets overseeing 25 men each ('companies of 50, each company officered by a Captain and two Lieutenants', was how Graham translated it to his father). However, they were slow and in some cases reluctant to muster; while the use of Cape Regiment troops to compensate for the initial poor turnout merely exacerbated the problem.[10]

Graham was aware that he could not treat the Boers as if they were simply an extension of the British army. When misunderstandings arose, he therefore took care to defuse the situation. 'I thought their being made acquainted with some certain parts of a little book entitled "Articles of War" would do no harm', he explained to his father at one point, 'and I had it translated and read to them accordingly.' But it was a serious error. 'This frightened some of them prodigiously', he observed, 'and some well inclined person, who, luckily for his skin, I cannot discover, circulated a report, either through ignorance or malice, that they were all to be made soldiers of.' Had 'you seen me exerting my Dutch eloquence from the summit of a dunghill', he added, 'with a view to quiet the fears of and inspire with confidence the mob of uncouth figures, who surrounded the rostrum, you most assuredly could not have stood it'.

---

8   Lieutenant General Cradock to Lieutenant Colonel Graham, 6 Oct. 1811: C.T. Atkinson (ed.), *Manuscripts of Robert Graham Esq. of Fintry*, p.85.

9   Graham to Robert Graham, 12th of Fintry, 4 Oct. 1811 and 14 Feb. 1812: C.T. Atkinson (ed.), *Manuscripts of Robert Graham Esq. of Fintry*, pp.83, 105; Maclennan, *Proper Degree of Terror*, pp.81, 89. See also M. Streak, *The Afrikaner as Viewed by the English 1795–1854* (Cape Town: Struik, 1974).

10 Maclennan, *Proper Degree of Terror*, pp.89–90; Graham to Robert Graham, 12th of Fintry, 14 Feb. 1812: C.T. Atkinson (ed.), *Manuscripts of Robert Graham Esq. of Fintry*, p.106.

However, it had to be done. Two burghers who went so far as to 'desert' as a result of the rumour were even brought back and publicly pardoned.

Making light of the episode to his father, Graham was in fact in all seriousness, seeing the current campaign (as Clausewitz would presently formulate) as the continuation of politics by other means. He was looking beyond the cessation of hostilities. 'I have every reason to believe that this expedition will be the means of attaching [the frontier Boers] to the English Government more than any other measure which could have been devised', he reflected; 'as they must see that the sole and ultimate object of the present armament is to secure to them the quiet and permanent possession of their houses and property.'[11]

Three divisions were drawn up to clear the frontier districts: a right division commanded by Major Cuyler, Landdrost of Uitenhage, a central division commanded by Captain George Fraser of the Cape Regiment, and a left or northern division commanded by Anders Stockenström, Landdrost of Graaff-Reinet and father of Andries (at that time an ensign in the Cape Regiment, acting as his father's ADC). The movement of these divisions began as early as 20 December 1811. However, fearful that the developing concentration to the south would leave his district exposed, Stockenström on 29 December resolved to speak to Graham in person. He never made it. Accompanied by an escort of 24 burghers and an interpreter, he encountered a number of imiDange Xhosa with whom he endeavoured to enter into a dialogue, only for his party to be surrounded and attacked. Stockenström and seven of his party were killed. (Among the dead was Jan Christiaan Greyling, whose widow would go on to marry the future Voortrekker leader, Piet Retief.) Continuing with his plans, Graham instructed the left division to join up with Fraser's central column, this being effected at Zokamma/Jokamma, some 10 miles north-east of the mouth of the Sunday's River, on 1 January 1812.

It led to a mixed force of 800 men: 30 Royal Artillery, 20 Light Dragoons, 400 Cape Regiment and 350 armed burghers. The following day, 2 January, a force coordinated into six companies comprising 60 armed burghers and 20 Cape Regiment regulars each, set out to sweep the Addo Forest. According to Johan de Villiers, the leading authority on this period of South African military history, this was the first time colonial troops were used 'to scour thickets systematically on foot in this frontier war'.[12]

It was difficult work, in which the Xhosa made good use of the terrain. After five days the exhausted companies returned to the combined division's base with 2,500 confiscated cattle and reports of between 12 and 14 Xhosa killed. This number included the sick and ageing Chungwa, chief of the Gqunukhwebe group, whose territory between the Sunday's and Fish rivers was the most vulnerable to predatory colonists.

---

11 Graham to Robert Graham, 12th of Fintry, 14 Feb. 1812: C.T. Atkinson (ed.), *Manuscripts of Robert Graham Esq. of Fintry*, pp.105–106.
12 J. de Villiers, 'Perspective', pp.41–42. On the death of Anders Stockenström note J. Laband, *The Land Wars: The Dispossession of the Khoisan and AmaXhosa in the Cape Colony* (Cape Town: Penguin, Random House, 2020), p.127, and DSAB I, p.774.

Xhosa hunting elephant along the Great Fish River (as reproduced by Cory, *Rise of South Africa* 1, 1910, from painting 'in possession of Rev. Dr. Flint, of Cape Town')

His death was not without controversy. As the colonial force approached his Great Place on 3 January, adherents lifted Chungwa from his sickbed and attempted to hide him in an inaccessible area of bush. However, a Boer patrol managed to follow the path, and on discovering Chungwa and a few followers asleep, reputedly shot them where they lay. Graham had no qualms, writing to his father on 14 February that Chungwa was 'fortunately one of the first who fell' and seeing it as having a salutary effect.

In return, Graham had to report the death of 'Veld Cornet Nortjie … killed by an assigay'. Indeed, he had 'much reason to be pleased with the conduct of the farmers' in general, he stated, adding (in contrast to his earlier views) that 'they are orderly, obedient, and undertake with cheerfulness and alacrity the fatiguing and arduous duties necessarily allotted to them'.[13]

Nonetheless, realising that the expulsion of the Xhosa and its aftermath was going to be considerably more problematic than he had anticipated, Graham on 8 January 1812 requested the transfer of at least 200 regular troops as reinforcements. Cradock, a man of considerable military experience, responded with the embarkation of nine officers, 10 NCOs, four drummers and 200 rank and file of the 60th Regiment of Foot, who arrived on the frontier in February.[14]

---

[13] Graham to Lieutenant Colonel T. Reynell, Military Secretary, 8 Jan. 1812; Graham to Robert Graham, 12th of Fintry, 14 Feb. 1812: C.T. Atkinson (ed.), *Manuscripts of Robert Graham Esq. of Fintry*, pp.93–94, 104; Maclennan, *Proper Degree of Terror*, p.112; N. Etherington, *The Great Treks: The Transformation of Southern Africa, 1815–1854* (London: Longman, 2001), pp.61–63.

[14] Cradock to Graham, 18 Jan. 1812: C.T. Atkinson (ed.), *Manuscripts of Robert Graham Esq. of Fintry*, pp.96–97.

BACKGROUND: THE EASTERN FRONTIER

There were further frustrations, as when on 10 January a party of Xhosa attacked the farm of 'Van de Merwe under Bamboos Berg' and murdered his wife, and on 11 and 12 January, when several parties 'entered different parts of the Hoegte' and 'owing to the pusilanimity [sic] of the individuals intrusted [sic] with the command of patrols of Boers in that quarter, succeeded in murdering two Hottentot herd[er]s and driving off a considerable number of cattle'. However, when need arose Graham would not hesitate to discipline Boers who neglected their duties.

'The most conspicuous instance of misconduct', he reported to Henry Alexander, the Colonial Secretary to the Cape Government, on 30 January 1812, was that of *Hemraad* Christoffel Lombard, resident at Bruinjes Hoegte,

> who ... permitted, it is supposed, 20 or 30 Kaffers and four Hottentots with guns to drive off the whole of his cattle, 208 in number, in broad day, without taking proper measures to prevent them, though he had 30 armed men on his place, a few of whom only were sent by him after the robbers ... he remaining at home with the remainder of his force.

Hottentot (Khoikhoi) soldier, Cape Regiment. (Museum Africa, previously Africana Museum)

Graham contrasted this with the 'conduct of the farmer Louis Nel', who had demonstrated that what Graham called (in an official communication) 'the savages' (that is, Xhosa) are 'easily intimidated by spirited conduct'. Graham immediately 'dismissed Lombard from the situation of *Hemraad* and Captain' and granted Louis Nel 'his loan place free of rent for 10 years'.[15]

One cannot but highlight the strange dichotomy to be found in Graham's description of these Xhosa marauders ('savages') as against the affectionate, if paternal, reference to the men of the Cape Regiment ('my own lads'). Just as his invective against the first knew no limits, describing them to Cradock's Military Secretary, Thomas Reynell, as 'these horrid savages' ('notwithstanding the panegyrics of Mr. John Barrow', as he later added to his father), so he could not praise the latter too highly. 'I cannot pass over in silence the remarkable good [sic] behaviour of the men of the Cape Regiment', he reported to Reynell; 'they have answered my most sanguine expectations and the good opinion I ever entertained of them.'[16] Nor, whatever he might say

---

15 Graham to H. Alexander, 30 Jan. 1812: C.T. Atkinson (ed.), *Manuscripts of Robert Graham Esq. of Fintry*, p.98.
16 Graham to Lieutenant Colonel T. Reynell, 31 Jan. 1812; Graham to Robert Graham, 12th of Fintry, 14 Feb. 1812: C.T. Atkinson (ed.), *Manuscripts of Robert Graham Esq. of Fintry*, pp.100–101, 107.

CONTROLLING THE FRONTIER

Portrait of a Xhosa chief, ascribed to a dragoon officer in the force under Graham's command. (*A Collection of Portraits of the Savage Tribes inhabiting the Boundaries of the Colony of the Cape of Good Hope. Taken from Life in 1812, by an Officer of the 21st Lt. Dragoons, engaged in an Expedition against those Tribes, under Lt. Col. Graham*, McQueen & Co., lithograph, published by Edwd. Orme, Bond St, London, 1822)

at any given moment in his frustration, were these Xhosa 'easily intimidated by spirited conduct', or he would not at that time have been requesting the transfer of regular troops as reinforcements.

Nonetheless, by the time of the 60th Foot's arrival, Graham's scorched earth tactics had begun to take effect. Indeed, by the end of February, Graham was reporting that the frontier districts had effectively been cleared of Xhosa and that the focus was now on measures to ensure the continued stability of the region.[17]

To understand why the 60th Foot was such an important augmentation of Graham's force at this time, some explanation is necessary.

---

17 J. de Villiers, 'Perspective', pp.42–44.

BACKGROUND: THE EASTERN FRONTIER

First appearance of the 60th Regiment

The purpose of the 60th (Royal American) Regiment had been to combine the qualities of the scout with the discipline of the trained soldier, in the manner of the light troops of Marshal de Saxe. As such, the military historian and theorist, J.F.C. Fuller, could describe the 60th as 'the first true light infantry the British Standing Army ever had'. The predominant foreign element upon its founding – Swiss, Tyrolese and Germans, recruited in large measure in Pennsylvania – constituted a positive benefit, for these recruits were noted hunters and Indian fighters, superb frontiersmen, who established themselves as masters of forest warfare.[18] More recently a 5th Battalion of the regiment, raised in 1797, was the first British unit to be dressed wholly in green and to be armed with the rifle as standard; and this battalion became the first unit ashore at Mondego Bay when Wellington landed in Portugal in 1808. Yet the 1st Battalion won no such credit and, notwithstanding its frontier origins, was transferred to the Cape as a form of penal battalion.

Why? There is no great mystery in reality. This state of affairs developed primarily out of the deleterious effects of a prolonged period of service in the West Indies, where the battalion will have been associated with the Royal African Corps' sister units, and where its foreign legion ethos had become increasingly coloured by penal based recruitment. However, this expedient method of recruitment was not confined to its period of service in the West Indies. When the 1st Battalion returned to the UK it was in order to remain as a 'foreign-legion', but with its ranks drawn from prisoners of war. And a quick turnaround it was. As the regiment's official history records briskly:

> The 1st Battalion, having handed over to other battalions all its efficient men, quitted Maroontown in Jamaica and was sent home in 1810 to Hilsea, where the Colonel-Commandant, General Whetham (at that time Lieut.-Governor of Portsmouth), filled up its ranks from the prisoners of war (excepting those of French birth) to be found in the neighbourhood. From Hilsea the battalion went to Cowes whence, on 30 May, 1811, it embarked (1,000 strong) for the Cape of Good Hope.[19]

And yet there was nothing unusual in this practice, and nor was there anything particularly out of the ordinary in the first years of the battalion's deployment along the Cape frontier. Arriving at Algoa Bay on 3 February 1812, the initial danger the regiment faced did not in fact result from its deployment on the frontier, but rather its hazardous disembarkation at the bay. A boat was 'upset in landing the troops', two soldiers drowned and the others in the boat were only saved when some men of the 83rd, 'at the risk of their own lives, swam through the surf and brought them safe on shore'.

---

18 J.F.C. Fuller, *British Light Infantry in the Eighteenth Century* (London: Hutchinson, 1925), pp.97–110.
19 L. Butler, *The Annals of the King's Royal Rifle Corps: Volume 1, 'The Royal Americans'* (London: Smith, Elder & Co., 1913), pp.282-283.

Clearing the bush, from a lithograph by the Grahamstown artist Frederick Timpson I'Ons. (I'Ons was a volunteer in the Sixth Frontier War of 1834-35)

In his report Graham commended Captain Cameron of the 83rd for 'his exertion and judgement' in safely disembarking the rest.[20]

The 60th consequently arrived during the later stages of the Fourth Cape Frontier War, being moved up to relieve four companies of the Cape Regiment 'on the line of the defence', the latter then proceeding 'to join the main body in the field' prior to the systematic clearing of the Zuurberg. The force available until then had not been 'sufficiently numerous effectually to scour', Graham noted; but now the 'whole disposeable [sic] force' gathered on the evening of 12 February, and at daybreak on 13th 'were detached on foot in two divisions, one on the North and the other on [the] South side [of] the mountain … scouring every kloof.' The whole force returned to Colonel Graham's position at Rietberg on 24 February.[21]

This was certainly an unpleasant operation – Graham himself described it as 'detestible [sic] work' as 'we are forced to hunt them like wild beasts' – but it effectively finished the campaign to clear the region and establish the Great Fish River as the colonial frontier. Hardly 'a trace of a Caffer man remains', he subsequently reported; all seen had been 'killed and wounded' to 'the number [of] about 30', while '[u]pwards of 100 women and children' were taken and repatriated.

---

20   Graham to Lieutenant Colonel T. Reynell, 26 Feb. 1812: C.T. Atkinson (ed.), *Manuscripts of Robert Graham Esq. of Fintry*, p.108.
21   Ibid.

BACKGROUND: THE EASTERN FRONTIER

Regarding causalities for the campaign as a whole, Graham acknowledged to his father that '[w]e have had a few men killed and wounded'. On the other hand, 'I should think about 300 Kaffers may have been killed and a good many wounded', he surmised; adding, circumspectly, that 'with African Boers and Hottentots, contrary to what is usual, the number of killed much exceeds that of wounded'. Far from being seen as unsuitable for this work, the new intake of the 60th would appear to have been chosen specifically to remain on the frontier during the period in which Graham thereafter sought to establish a chain of fortified posts along it.

The aim was that the indigenous Cape Regiment would then be stationed permanently on the frontier, having the support of those British units deployed in the Cape – the 83rd Foot, the 21st Light Dragoons, and in particular the Cape Regiment's recently arrived sister light infantry unit, the 60th Regiment – at least until such time as stability was, as it was hoped, firmly established.[22]

Such odium as did over time come to be associated with the 'detestable work' of the campaign derived instead more from those in command, and notably from the laconic and, initially, anything but didactic journal entries of Colonel Graham's highly experienced and competent adjutant, Lieutenant Robert Hart. This was not without a certain irony, for the irrepressible Hart was a devout Scottish Presbyterian, who would presently become a widely respected and philanthropically inclined member of the frontier community. Not least he would superintend the Government farm at what became Somerset East and establish a close friendship with the Scottish 1820 Settler and anti-slavery campaigner Thomas Pringle.

Thomas Pringle (1789-1834): 1820 Settler, journalist, poet, humanitarian and Whig leaning activist. (Stipple and line engraving by William Finden, published by Edward Moxon, Dover Street, London, 1837)

But characteristically, just as his journal of the recent campaign had not shied away from many of its more unpleasant and controversial details, so equally he would subsequently openly share the manuscript with the sympathetic and inquisitive Pringle. As a result extracts appeared in Pringle's *Narrative of a Residence in South Africa* published in 1834 ('I have now lying before me a journal, kept during [the] campaign by my friend Mr. Hart', Pringle states in the book), and this led to the relevant extracts being still more dramatically highlighted in *The Wrongs of the Caffre Nation*, issued in 1837 under the *nom de plume* 'Justus'. 'Justus' was believed to have been the pro-philanthropic Grahamstown surgeon and journalist, A.G. Campbell,

---

22 Lieutenant Colonel T. Reynell to Graham, 7 Feb. 1812; Graham to Robert Graham, 12th of Fintry, 14 Feb. 1812; Graham to Lieutenant Colonel T. Reynell, 26 Feb. 1812: C.T. Atkinson (ed.), *Manuscripts of Robert Graham Esq. of Fintry*, pp.101–102, 105, 108; Maclennan, *Proper Degree of Terror*, pp.131–132.

whose account of the death of the Xhosa paramount Hintsa in 1835 had by then already had important repercussions.[23]

The founding of Grahamstown

Graham was expecting to relinquish the command at the close of the campaign, and was concerned that his beloved creation (the term is used advisedly), the Cape Regiment, was properly recognised and provided for. He could not praise his Khoi soldiers ('my poor fellows, the Hottentots') too highly, almost like the way that Sikh soldiers would come to be viewed in the Raj, and went so far as to state to his father that they were every bit as good as Europeans, both as troops and – once the prejudice was stripped away – men. Experience of the campaign had 'far surpassed' his hopes and expectations ('my opinion of them, though contrary to that of several Great Men, was well grounded', he asserted). However, the only way that the prejudice could be stripped away, to his mind, was to present them as Christians – or at least potential Christians.

In this respect, for all his genuine efforts, Graham was prone to a little exaggeration. 'Many of them have made such progress in religious knowledge through the medium of the Chaplain (a Dutch Missionary), who it was one of my first steps to provide, that they have', he stated, 'been baptised and are really good Christians.' This was a reference to the work of A.A. van der Lingen. Born in the Netherlands in 1774, Van der Lingen had come to the Cape as a missionary and worked for a time with Dr J.T. van der Kemp at Graaff-Reinet, before becoming chaplain to the Cape Regiment in 1806. In that role he also taught the Khoikhoi to read and write, but he did not enjoy the best of health and felt restricted in his work by the fact that, as Cape Malays, many of his soldiers were Muslim. Nonetheless, there was not 'a cleaner parade in the service than that of the Cape Regiment', Graham insisted, 'so let the Hottentots be no longer despised'.[24]

It was primarily in order to provide a frontier headquarters for the Cape Regiment that Sir John Cradock instructed Graham to identify the most suitable site for a new settlement. Graham lost little time, and as early as March 1812 accepted a recommendation that an abandoned farm on the banks of the Noutoe River (rather more accurately described by Stockenström as 'a weak stream'), which had long served as an outspan post for early Trekboers and travellers, was best placed for the purpose. But on closer inspection he became convinced that a more advantageous location was still to be found, and therefore ordered his trusted adjutant, Lieutenant

---

23 Thomas Pringle, *Narrative of a Residence in South Africa* (Cape Town: Struik edition, 1966), pp.274–275; A.L. Harington, *The Graham's Town Journal and The Great Trek, 1834–1843* (Johannesburg: Archives Year Book, Die Staatsdrukker, 1973), p.30; G.E. Cory, *The Rise of South Africa: A History of the Origin of South African Colonisation and of its Development Towards the East from the Earliest Times to 1857*, Vol. III (London: Longmans, Green & Co., 1919), pp.320–321; DSAB III, p.123.
24 Graham to Robert Graham, 12th of Fintry, 14 Feb. 1812: C.T. Atkinson (ed.), *Manuscripts of Robert Graham Esq. of Fintry*, pp.106–107; DSAB I, pp. 811–812.

BACKGROUND: THE EASTERN FRONTIER

Robert Hart, to join the officer in charge of the detachment fortifying the Noutoe position, Captain Donald McNeil, in further reconnoitring the surrounding area. They were to be accompanied by the young Andries Stockenström.

Stockenström recorded in his autobiography how he had arrived at the Noutoe location a few days before Colonel Graham in order that he might, as instructed, 'so thoroughly … have reconnoitred the country as to be able to show him the various locations for military posts'. Graham presently rode in, accompanied by the Deputy QMG, Cape Colony, Lieutenant Colonel Thomas Arbuthnot, and Captain Wallace of the 21st Dragoons. The current site was then inspected, for the work was well advanced, and a few days' rest gained, before at some point on or about 4 May Graham duly ordered Stockenström to 'escort him over the vicinity'.[25]

By then Stockenström had a particular site in mind, bearing in mind the wider strategic context: the abandoned farm *De Rietfontein* or *De Twee Fontijnen*, which lay some seven miles to the south. De Rietfontein had lately belonged to one Lucas Meyer (and the farm was indeed called by Stockenström 'Lucas Meyers'), but there does not seem to have been any contemporary claimant. One may speculate as to why, the more especially because, although some years dead, this Lucas Meyer had been a far from insignificant frontiersman. But the answer may lie in the name. It is possible, although by no means certain, that this Meyer was the same man who had participated in the 1799 Graaff-Reinet rebellion. Either way the name had long been notorious on the frontier.

Hottentot (Khoikhoi) bugle boy, Cape Regiment, sketched by ensign R.H. Dingley, October 1816. (Museum Africa, previously Africana Museum)

Stockenström's extended autobiography, it may be admitted, is hardly written in the most riveting style. However, in detailing the events of that long day spent traversing the frontier country in company with Colonel Graham, the likely mood comes across all the more vividly for being conveyed with both dryness and understatement:

> I took [Colonel Graham] direct to an old farm called Lucas Meyers [that is, called Lucas Meyer's farm], which had been abandoned by the owner, and burnt by the

---

25 C.W. Hutton (ed.), *The Autobiography of the late Sir Andries Stockenström, Bart*, Vol. I (Cape Town: J.C. Juta & Co., 1887/ Cape Town: Struik, facs. reproduction, 1964), pp.62–63.

Kaffirs; thence he ascended the southern ridge, whence he had a complete view of the coast and the lower part of the Fish River to its mouth. We next returned to the old kraals, examined the springs, then galloped across the flat to the Governor's Kop, then called 'Rand Kop', where he had a most extensive view of the Keiskamma, the Tyumie, the Kat, Koonap, and North Kowie Mountains, as well as the upper Fish River as far as Esterhuis Poort. I pointed out to him the exact position of Trompetter's Drift and Hermanus Kraal, but humbly suggested that Meyers [sic] was a more commanding position. He objected to the weakness of the water. I knew none stronger in the country. We galloped back to Meyers, then off-saddled and took some refreshment under a tree now near the centre of Graham's Town.[26]

Graham on this occasion would appear to have been positing negatives in the manner of devil's advocate, exploring any weak features of the location to counterbalance Stockenström's persuasive advocacy of its benefits. Moreover, during the interlude it is likely that Graham was weighing up the options. Certainly he will have consulted his staff, not least Lieutenant Hart (who was much more closely involved in the entire procedure than Stockenström allows) and Captain McNeil, as well as Ensign Stockenström; and they, perhaps more than Stockenström, would have been privy to the extent to which he was in fact already persuaded.

In any event Stockenström was not for long left in the dark. Remounting, the party again 'ascended some high land overlooking the country and the coast', and after further engaging in 'some discussion with the members of his staff', as Stockenström recalled, Graham openly acknowledged that he preferred the current location to that of Noutoe. 'It is a pity', he added wistfully, 'so much has been done there'. But that was as maybe. 'At any rate', he made clear, 'here we must have our headquarters immediately, and let those old walls', he indicated with regard to Meyer's deserted farmhouse, 'be covered in for the officers' mess'.[27]

No one needed reminding of where that house was situated. It lay close by the mimosa tree under which they had recently rested. And legend has it that that site is today marked by the Grahamstown Centenary Memorial, standing to the front of Grahamstown Cathedral, which together with Church Square to the rear occupies the site of what had been Meyer's house and the first – improvised – officers' mess.

Together with the mess being made habitable, stables and other outhouses were quickly added, and further plans initiated. When Graham had spoken of the work being undertaken 'immediately' he meant exactly that: with winter fast approaching there was no small sense of urgency. The majority of the Cape Regiment were ordered down on 6 May, within a day or two of the decision to relocate being taken. The men were initially accommodated in tents and huts parallel with the mess, but already plots were identified on which to build small houses for the officers – including such prominent figures as Lieutenant Hart, Major George Fraser and the regiment's surgeon,

---

26 Hutton (ed.), *Stockenström*, I, p.63.
27 Hutton (ed.), *Stockenström*, I, p.63.

BACKGROUND: THE EASTERN FRONTIER

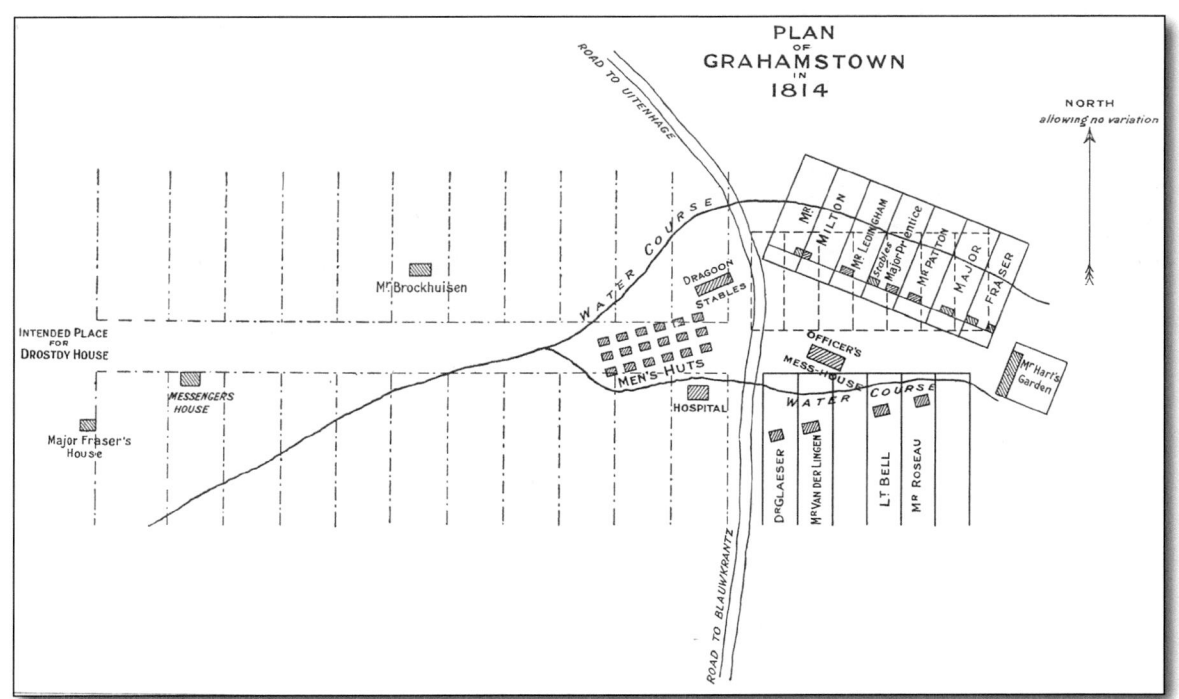

Plan of Grahamstown in 1814.
(Cory, *Rise of South Africa* 1)

W.W. Milton. These plots were sited to the east of the farmhouse/mess, in what is now the area of Church Square. Moreover the officers' stake in the settlement was strengthened still further when the governor subsequently made an official grant of the plots to the officers concerned.

There also arose the question of the garrison/settlement's name. The farm may previously have been called De Rietfonteine or Twee Fontijnen, but it would appear to have long been known colloquially simply as 'Meyers', which was never going to be thought appropriate or sufficient as the settlement broadened; and indeed, with the emerging military headquarters and developing habitation it is easy to imagine how the site might already have come to be referred to as 'Graham's Town', for it had been chosen on his authority. Either way, the following August 'Graham's Town' was formally recognised as the settlement's name 'in testimony of His Excellency's [Governor Sir John Cradock's] respect for the services of Lieut.-Colonel Graham, through whose spirited exertions', as the proclamation had it, 'the Caffre hordes have been driven from that valuable district'.[28]

It was to become the most important trading and administrative centre in the eastern Cape, and as such would in time come to exert a decisive influence on developments not only in the frontier region but also, little as it may have been anticipated, well beyond it.

---

28   J. de Villiers, 'Perspective', p.45; Maclennan, *Proper Degree of Terror*, pp.132–133, 148; C.T. Atkinson (ed.), *Manuscripts of Robert Graham Esq. of Fintry*, p.126.

CONTROLLING THE FRONTIER

An example of the earliest properties built with the establishment of Grahamstown. (Cory, *Rise of South Africa* 1, from painting 'in possession of Rev. Dr. Flint, of Cape Town')

Call for troop reductions

It had, as seen, been Colonel Graham's intention and understanding that the British units deployed in the recent war would remain on the frontier even as a line of strategically sited military posts were being constructed for its defence and the Cape Regiment was being embedded in the new garrison town. But with the Xhosa removed from the Zuurveld and the frontier established along the Great Fish River – or in other words, with the establishment of, as it was hoped, peace, no matter how tenuous or theoretical – there arose bureaucratic demands for economies. Such demands were both inevitable and predicable, and neither Cradock nor any other governor could remain impervious to them. The only question to be addressed was, were such demands premature? And if so, then to what extent, and what compromise or expedient could be effected to ameliorate the situation?

Thus as early as March 1812 Cradock proposed returning the frontier detachment of the 83rd to Cape Town. This would still leave Graham two companies of the 60th, a detachment of the 21st Dragoons and an artillery attachment; but for how much longer? For not only was it made clear that even these units were being retained with some reluctance, and for a limited, if as yet indeterminate, period; it was equally understood that Graham should be working actively towards achieving a situation in which they could be expeditiously withdrawn. As Cradock's military secretary, Lieutenant Colonel Reynell, conveyed it in a letter of 6 March:

> His Excellency trusts, that these latter may be [maintained] upon as reduced a scale as circumstances can possibly admit, and he also indulges the hope that the service of the detachment of the 60th Regiment may be dispensed with, if not immediately, at least in the course of a few months.[29]

---

29 Lieutenant Colonel T. Reynell to Graham, 6 March 1812: C.T. Atkinson (ed.), *Manuscripts of Robert Graham Esq. of Fintry*, p.110.

The tone of the communication was anything but peremptory, and reflected Cradock's confidence in Graham's judgement, just as Graham in turn felt sufficiently secure in the governor's confidence to argue the point. With the Xhosa still restive and the dark winter nights approaching, now was not the time to begin reducing the force deployed along the frontier, he insisted, just as Cradock had no doubt anticipated that he would. Cradock was sympathetic. Nonetheless, the issue had to be addressed, and there was give and take on both sides.[30] Just one troop of cavalry was recalled together with the artillery detachment, while a fresh troop of dragoons was sent up to relieve the remainder, who had in fact by then effectively ceased to operate as cavalry as a result of a periodic outbreak of distemper.

For all that, nothing had really changed. It was still a case of withdrawal 'if not immediately, at least in the course of a few months'. Over the longer term the defence of the frontier would have to depend, at least in the first instance, upon the colony's domestic resources.

Graham's 'Instructions to Commanders of Posts'

By mid May 1812 the participating Boer commandos had also been released, but only to be replaced by a fresh contingent of some 300 burghers drawn from as wide afield as Graaff-Reinet, Swellendam, Stellenbosch and George; and together with the Cape Regiment these men were to continue the work of patrolling the frontier. To secure that contested frontier with the diminishing resources available it would be necessary, as Graham made plain, not only as far as possible to meet, but still more to deter, any prospective infringements. In other words, it would be necessary to instil a sense of fear among the frontier Xhosa – or rather a continued sense of fear, following on from the systematic expulsion of the Xhosa from the Zuurveld. There was no room for ambiguity: any future border violation would have to be met with the utmost severity.

Thorough and considered in all his preparations, Graham had indeed already gone to some lengths to ensure that those charged with the day-to-day defence of the frontier understood both what was expected of them and the dangers and difficulties to which they would be exposed. From Uitenhage – where the landdrost, Cuyler, had up to the establishment of Grahamstown, held responsibility for the border district stretching right across to the Fish River – Graham had, on 30 March, issued a communication headed 'Instructions to Commanders of Posts'. Much quoted, it was essentially a summation of the skills needed in this form of bush warfare or confrontation (albeit the situation was now more in the nature of a standoff), evolving out of, but not entirely confined to, the experience of the Cape frontier; such methods having, as noted, been mastered by the 60th Regiment on a different frontier some half century before.

---

30 Lieutenant Colonel T. Reynell to Graham, 31 March 1812: C.T. Atkinson (ed.), *Manuscripts of Robert Graham Esq. of Fintry*, pp.111–112.

Above all, the document asserted that the defence of the frontier must needs be proactive, with the troops deployed having as their first duty not simply to patrol but, more particularly, systematically to observe and scour every wood or bush in which the Xhosa might conceivably find concealment. The greater part of the text comprised practical advice as how best to achieve that aim: these were the 'instructions' to which the title referred. Throughout there are echoes of Bouquet's earlier instructions to the 60th Royal American Regiment, and of the practice of irregular frontier warfare more generally, not least when Graham prefaces his directives with the observation that: 'As so much depends on locality, unforeseen circumstances, etc., a great deal is left to the judgement and discretion of officers and non-coms [NCOs].'

With that as a given, Graham enumerated in quick succession those particulars that must be 'strictly adhered to'. Thus, both officers and men should make themselves 'perfectly acquainted with the country between their post and the next in every direction, and have a thorough knowledge of all roads, paths, kloofs, etc.' That both officers and men were to 'guard against surprise' and were 'to carry guns when going for wood, water, etc.' ('Experience has shown that no mercy is to be expected from the Kaffirs', he warned; 'they are very cunning and only attack … when their enemy is off their guard'.) That troops were to blend into their surroundings, both visually and as far as possible audibly, and be prepared to do so at a moment's notice. 'Nothing white is ever to appear on any man required to turn out at night', it was stipulated. 'If a post is attacked the men are to turn out without noise or confusion and all regularity. No man to fire unless sure of his aim and never more than half the party to be unloaded at once.' But then nor were the enemy ever to be pursued at night 'except in moonlight and in open country'. All bushes in the immediate vicinity of a post should in any case have been 'cleared away'.

On the subject of patrolling Graham was equally prescriptive. 'Frequent' patrols were to be sent out from each post, he stated; but while their precise strength would be dependent upon both terrain and numbers available, certain observances were again to be strictly adhered to:

> Patrols to be perfectly silent and to conceal themselves as much as possible. Parties when concealing themselves at places where Kaffirs are likely to pass, are not to make a fire. Spoors of men and beasts are to be studied by all, and every man is to accustom himself to look for them. Notice to be instantly given of the trace of any fresh Kaffir spoor to the officer commanding, and this to be followed until it is ascertained that it passes out of the neighbourhood of the post. On traces discovered going westward, notice to be given to the posts best situated to overtake or intercept the invaders. On such notice being received every effort must be made to overtake the Kaffirs. Any of the men going about without shoes to make a cross here and there on their tracks in order to show that it is the track of a friend – the sign to be occasionally changed as required. An escort of infantry to escort orderly dragoons when danger is apprehended.

Lastly, there was the question of the settlers. White settlement (Boer or European) in the newly pacified, if still unstable, region was sparse, and likely to remain so for some years yet; but the hope and expectation was that new settlers would, with help, begin to take root, multiply, form settled communities and eventually thrive. Their protection was therefore seen to be imperative, and formed the subject of the final raft of Graham's directives.

'The families and property of the inhabitants is under the protection of the troops', Graham reminded his post commanders, 'and every assistance is to be rendered them. If necessary', he added, 'a guard must assist in guarding the flocks [sic], particularly at night': a duty 'to be particularly attended to by the posts along the Great Fish River'. He then specified the procedures to be followed upon a report of missing livestock. They were stark and undeviating. 'On notice of theft of cattle, immediate notice is to be sent from post to post towards the frontier and every effort made to recover them', he stated: 'All Kaffirs and their followers seen within the limits [are] to be considered as enemies and dealt with accordingly'.

The only exception to this rule would be in the case of those Xhosa 'bearing communications from their chiefs'. But then, if genuine, they should not be roaming freely, for the only official crossing-place was at what Graham called 'William Van Aardt's ford' on the Fish River. George Cory, in quoting this passage in 1910, noted *in parenthesis* that the ford was 'near the present Longhope Siding': adding that 'the district of Bedford was then Kaffirland'. William Van Aardt's ford had long been of significance to Boer and Xhosa alike, and was, in fact, earmarked as the site of the most northerly of the frontier posts to which Graham referred. And it is worth turning to the foldout map at the back of Cory's volume to note its position – a little below Cookhouse, Esterhuis Poort and Slagter's Nek (or 'Slachtersnek', as the Boers spelt it).

The 'instructions' concluded by confirming that all prisoners apprehended were still, in this period before the as yet unnamed settlement of Grahamstown was properly established, 'to be well secured and forwarded to Uitenhage'. 'All Hottentots [Khoikhoi] and slaves without passes found at a distance from a dwelling and not giving a satisfactory answer', Graham added, in conformity with the already controversial Caledon Code, were 'to be dealt with as Kaffirs.'[31]

The reality behind Graham's 'Instructions'

Graham was in fact being circumspect: in reality, he was prepared to go further than outlined in this document. When he wrote that 'every effort' should be made to recover stolen cattle, he meant not just up to the river frontier, but if necessary beyond it. The Xhosa should not feel safe from the consequences of their actions simply by crossing over the Fish River: if

---

31 G.E. Cory, *Rise of South Africa*, Vol. I (London: Longmans, Green & Co., 1910), pp.252–253; E. and J. Gledhill, *In the Steps of Piet Retief* (Cape Town: Human & Rousseau, 1980), p.43; Maclennan, *Proper Degree of Terror*, pp.134–135; N. Mostert, *Frontiers: The Epic of South Africa's Creation and the Tragedy of the Xhosa People* (New York: Alfred A. Knopf, 1992), p.391; Fuller, *British Light Infantry*, pp.102, 106–107.

anything, the severity beyond the frontier had, for both practical and political reasons, to be starker still. Thus patrols in pursuit of stolen cattle were not only sanctioned to cross over the frontier, they were also directed to 'fire on all Kaffirs who oppose them'.

The initiative – and indeed initial authority – for this potentially dangerous and provocative procedure came from Graham. But when communicating with the governor he at no time sought to dissemble or misrepresent his aims. Whatever the 'instructions' may have said about all prisoners being 'well secured and forwarded to Uitenhage', encroaching Xhosa were in fact to be shot on sight: no prisoners were be taken. 'To take plundering Kaffers prisoners is impossible', he stated; 'if they are not fired on their numbers will encrease [sic], [and] with numbers audacity'. Upon it being spelt out, Cradock fully supported Graham's stance.[32]

However, it would not be Graham who oversaw the maintenance of frontier defences over the coming years. Anxious to return to Great Britain, he left 'the Frontier Head Quarters near Fish River' in June 1812 and, 'after a ride of 700 miles or so … accomplished in eight days and nights', arrived back in Cape Town on 1 July.[33]

Before he left, Graham 'set out … to take one more look at and bid farewell' to the Cape Regiment. It was an emotional occasion. 'Never shall I forget the looks of my poor Hottentots when they saw me going away' (he 'could not help' mentioning to his father); 'not until then, I believe, had they or I any idea of the mutual love we bore each other'. And '[n]o wonder!' he exclaimed. He had found them, he said, 'miserably oppressed', and since then had 'stood forth as their champion on every occasion' – by which he meant 'not those of the regiment alone', but generally –'and well has my trouble been repaid'. After a final inspection, and finding everything 'to my perfect satisfaction at the different military posts', Graham finally set out for Uitenhage on 19 June, and from there to Cape Town on 23 June 1812.[34]

Back in Europe he served for a time in Holland as military secretary and aide-de-camp to his kinsman, General Sir Thomas Graham (raised to the peerage as Lord Lynedoch in May 1814), participating in the unsuccessful attack on Bergen-op-Zoom on 8 March 1814, concerning which he left a detailed account.[35] But it was always his intention to return to the Cape, and this he did in 1815. Upon his return, with Lord Charles Somerset in place as governor, he accepted the post of commandant of Simon's Town.

---

32 Maclennan, *Proper Degree of Terror*, pp.135–136; Graham to Lieutenant Colonel T. Reynell, 15 May 1812; Lieutenant Colonel T. Reynell to Graham, 23 May 1812: C.T. Atkinson (ed.), *Manuscripts of Robert Graham Esq. of Fintry*, pp.121–122, 124.
33 Graham to Robert Graham, 12th of Fintry, 1 July 1812: C.T. Atkinson (ed.), *Manuscripts of Robert Graham Esq. of Fintry*, p.125.
34 Graham to Robert Graham, 12th of Fintry, 15 Aug. 1812: C.T. Atkinson (ed.), *Manuscripts of Robert Graham Esq. of Fintry*, p.127.
35 C.T. Atkinson (ed.), *Manuscripts of Robert Graham Esq. of Fintry*, pp.194–199.

BACKGROUND: THE EASTERN FRONTIER

Earliest known picture of Grahamstown, reputedly painted by Thomas Philipps's wife, Charlotte, and thus after the arrival of the 1820 Settlers. The house of future Voortrekker leader Piet Retief is indicated centre right; the fighting in 1819 took place over the undulating ground to the left. (Albany Museum)

Conference at the Kat River

Lord Charles Somerset, who had been appointed governor of the Cape Colony in 1813, was only too aware of the continuing frontier unrest in the wake of the Boer Slachtersnek rebellion of 1815. Cognisant of the inadequate resources at his disposal, and the inability of the colony to sustain a protracted war on the eastern frontier, he determined to make an official visit and confer with Ngqika and the other Xhosa chiefs in an effort to establish a definite and agreed scheme for the peaceful administration of the region.

The governor's party arrived at the frontier early in March 1817, at which point instructions were sent to the LMS missionary, Joseph Williams, to convene a general meeting between the governor and the leading Xhosa chiefs. Having only arrived in the colony in 1815, Williams had established the first permanent mission station in 'Kaffraria' the year before, close to Ngqika on the Kat River (near present-day Port Beaufort). However, overcome with fear and doubts as to the purpose of such a meeting, Ngqika was reluctant to attend, as indeed were many other chiefs. Poor Williams, not for the last time, was placed in an invidious and potentially dangerous position: the Xhosa leaders had to be harried and cajoled over a period of two weeks; but eventually, on 2 April Ngqika, Ndlambe and the other chiefs arrived at the meeting ground on the Kat River, where they came upon a large white marquee before which sat Lord Charles Somerset surrounded by cavalry, infantry, field artillery and a 350 strong burgher commando.[36]

The Xhosa were overawed, as was the intention. Then after the formalities, there followed the conference, the purpose being, Somerset declared, to

---

36   Mostert, *Frontiers*, pp.429ff and 447–449; Hutton (ed.), *Stockenström*, I, pp.98–99.

CONTROLLING THE FRONTIER

Lord Charles Somerset, 1767-1831: Governor of the Cape, 1814-1826. (Pen and pencil sketch, National Library of South Africa, Cape Town)

renew friendship and put an end to livestock theft and the murder that so often went with it.

Somerset stipulated that both Ngqika and Ndlambe must share responsibility with the colonial administrators – present in the persons of Colonel Jacob Cuyler from Uitenhage, Andries Stockenström from Graaff-Reinet and Major George Fraser from Grahamstown – for the detection and punishment of cattle raiders. In practical terms, this meant that farmers from the colony would be entitled to claim compensation from the first Xhosa kraal to which the livestock were traced. They would report their losses to a military post, after which a patrol would follow the spoor to the first kraal over the Fish River, from which cattle compensating for the loss would then be taken, leaving the inhabitants to seek redress from their chief – who would, in theory, track down the thieves. This was the controversial 'spoor law' (or 'reprisal system', as it was sometimes called, according to Stockenström).

The law was based on Xhosa custom, but wide open to abuse on both sides of the frontier, and in promulgating it Somerset took little heed of the internecine rivalry between Ngqika and Ndlambe, still less the internal stresses of Xhosa dynastic culture more widely. He simply reinforced the policy of treating Ngqika as the paramount chief of the Xhosa nation – as if recognising him as such, and investing him with the governor's own authority, would thereby make it so. It did not. The other chiefs did not generally recognise Ngqika as paramount. Thus he had little or no control over them. He was again being invested with an authority that he was unable to maintain, including being burdened with the responsibility of issuing passes for those Xhosa wishing to enter the colony.[37]

---

37   Mostert, *Frontiers*, pp.450–451; Hutton (ed.), *Stockenström*, I, pp.99–103.

BACKGROUND: THE EASTERN FRONTIER

Meeting between Batavian military governor, J.W. Janssens, and Xhosa chief, Ngqika, at the Kat River in 1803. Lord Charles Somerset met the Xhosa chiefs Ngqika and Ndlambe in similar fashion in April 1817. (Aquatint published in Amsterdam in 1810 by Evert Maaskamp, from drawing by Paravicini di Capelli. Issued as an accompaniment to *De Kaffers aan de Zuidkust van Afrika* by former landdrost of Uitenhage and early European authority on the Xhosa, Johann Christoph Ludwig [Lodewijk] Alberti, 1768-1812)

2

The Fifth Cape Frontier War

The Royal African Corps in the Cape Colony

June 1817 saw the arrival of new troops at Cape Town. They were, however, no ordinary troops, and the commotion their arrival engendered was no ordinary commotion. These were the men of the Royal African Corps, together with hastily drafted support from the same source for the 1st Battalion, 60th Regiment.

The latter had, as seen, been deployed in the Cape Colony since 1812 with no particular difficulties; as always there was a crying need for garrison troops on the eastern frontier. So why, one may ask, should the arrival of these units have proved so contentious? A glance at their brief respective histories provides the answer.

The Royal African Corps originated with the need to garrison the west African island of Goree. The French had been trading on the Senegal River since the seventeenth century, and maintained two coastal bases: Saint-Louis, situated on an island at the river's mouth, and the Isle of Goree, located further down the coast. The latter was duly captured from the French in 1800. But like other west African colonies, such as Sierra Leone and the Gambia, the climate was so unhealthy as to make it a proverbial white man's graveyard. Few men with any choice would willingly stop there, and the War Office was itself reluctant to provide a regular garrison. Therefore they initiated a penal corps for the purpose. Originally raised in 1800 as 'Fraser's Corps of Infantry' (after it first colonel, the resolute John Fraser), it arrived in west Africa just two companies strong in January 1801, and became better known as the Goree Corps, before being renamed soon after as the African Corps.

It was in fact one of several 'condemned battalions' raised during the period, recruited in the main from among those deserters and criminals to be found in the nation's prison hulks, but with the gradual addition of a variable number of foreigners of dubious repute and of black soldiers. Thus, while prison sentences could be exchanged for service in west Africa or the West Indies, it is scarcely to be wondered that these formations were often (at least to begin with) an unsavoury and ill-disciplined lot. Certainly none can have had a more mixed reputation than the African Corps, in all its various guises.

Its first years were not without incident or, it must be said, credit: not that those involved had a great deal of choice in the matter. By August 1803, by which time it maintained on paper at least seven companies, there was a unit of just 59 all ranks deployed in Sierra Leone, and 98 at Goree, but when a superior French naval force attacked Goree in January 1804, they met with a spirited resistance. By the time Fraser was compelled to surrender on 18 January the enemy's losses exceeded the total strength of the garrison. It was, moreover, a short-lived victory. The French garrison in turn surrendered to the British on 9 March (after offering token resistance), and on 25 April, a 230 strong force of the restyled 'Royal African Corps' reoccupied the island.

It was from this force, under the helpful command of Major Richard Lloyd, that Lieutenant John Martyn and 35 men famously volunteered to accompany Mungo Park's official expedition along the course of the Niger in 1805. Park, a profound humanitarian, had been given a captain's commission for the purpose (his RAC jacket can still be seen in the Selkirk museum in Scotland), while the men were offered extra pay and the promise of a discharge on their return.[1] But, of course, none did return.

By that time the corps had a strength of 10 companies, but six stayed in England until being sent to the West Indies in October 1804, in addition to which there was the usual depletion through sickness. The strength was then increased to 12 companies the following year, after which, in October 1806, it was reconstituted as two separate corps of eight companies (theoretically composed of 100 men per company): one to retain the title Royal African Corps and serve in west Africa, the other to be styled the Royal West India Rangers and serve in the West Indies. However, even that quickly proved insufficient, so that in 1807 the Royal African Corps was increased to 10 companies and restyled the Royal York Rangers, with foreigners of European origin now accounting for 108 of the 265 NCOs and men on active service. Then in 1808, while based at Goree, this was itself reconstituted as two distinct corps, one retaining the name Royal York Rangers and being sent to the West Indies, and the other readopting the title Royal African Corps.

By 1809 the corps consisted predominantly of foreigners – 294 as against 102 British rank and file. In the desolate environment of west Africa the trend had little demonstrable effect on its short-term practical effectiveness: July 1809 saw 166 officers and men participate in the capture of Saint-Louis, in Senegal, while July 1814 saw an expedition along the Pongo to destroy slave-trading stations. The problem lay instead with the fearful mortality rate. A quarter of the deployment was dying every year from disease; which meant that an indefinite deployment was like waiting for death. It was that stark truth that lay behind the planned mutiny of a detachment in Senegal in 1810, which resulted in 25 men being executed and 25 more being 'exiled' to Sierra Leone.

Those men were not to know it, but the deployment was not in fact to be indefinite. So high was the mortality rate among white troops that with the ending of the Napoleonic wars it was decided to garrison the west

---

1   M. Duffill, *Mungo Park* (Edinburgh: NMS Publishing, 1999), pp.116–117.

African stations with black troops alone. Their proportion had also been progressively increasing, so that by 1813 there were as many as five black companies, comprising a total of some 475 soldiers (the majority recruited from the Liberated Africans Yard at Sierra Leone); but the number was rarely consistent from one year to the next. By February 1817, shortly before the post-war demarcation, there were in all 10 RAC companies, three of which were black. In the end six companies of Europeans were removed to the Cape Colony instead of remaining in west Africa. They arrived at the Cape, as seen, in June 1817.[2]

The precipitately drafted support for the 60th Regiment derived from similar materials as the RAC, and no doubt in earlier circumstances some at least would have been sent to garrison the west African stations with the RAC. But as it was, they would seem to have arrived at the Cape almost entirely without cohesion or effective discipline. Indeed, so acute was the problem that they were soon seen to represent a real danger to the maintenance of stability if deployed, as intended, along the eastern frontier.

What is clear is that – for both the RAC and the new draft of 1st 60th – the Cape Colony was politically and materially an altogether different world from their previous experience, one in which the rank and file felt strangely emancipated, for it placed them well beyond the harsh environmental restraints that had effectively dictated unit cohesion and discipline be it either in the West Indies or at Goree.

The negative impact on the Cape of both units, but of the 60th in particular, was immediate. The reinforcements of 1817 were of an altogether different order, and seen as such. Certainly the authorities were under no illusion as to calibre of troops arriving: stationed briefly in Simon's Town, the RAC fell under the authority of the town's commandant – none other than Colonel Graham. However even he experienced the greatest difficulty in dealing with them. He endeavoured to 'impress upon [the men's] minds the gratitude they ought to feel for their removal to the Cape', but gratitude did not come easily to such men. When the first batch had arrived it had been necessary to send guards aboard ship before they had so much as disembarked, and once on land, as Graham informed the governor Lord Charles Somerset's military secretary, Major George Rogers, their conduct was such 'as to cause constant alarm to the inhabitants'. Efforts were made to keep them under surveillance, but still, Graham reported, 'I do not think one day passed without some depredation or theft'. Certainly, he added, 'not a day passed on which many of them did not attempt to sell their necessaries. Every place of confinement was constantly full … during their stay'.

The precise extent of the 60th Regiment's indiscipline was detailed in a list drawn up in November 1817: no less than 12 men had been tried for the serious offence of striking a non-commissioned officer, 13 had deserted – six

---

2   R. Chartrand, *Émigré and Foreign Troops in British Service (2) 1803–15* (Oxford: Osprey, 2000), pp.35–36; Major J.J. Crooks, *Historical Records of the Royal African Corps* (Dublin: Browne & Nolan, 1925); W.Y. Baldry, 'Disbanded Regiments', *Journal of the Society for Army Historical Research* 14:56 (1935), pp.233–234; P.J. Haythornthwaite, *The Armies of Wellington* (London: Brockhampton Press, 1998), p.217.

THE FIFTH CAPE FRONTIER WAR

of whom had not been recaptured, 10 had been charged with being absent without leave, 11 with being drunk on guard, 22 with theft, 21 with the offence of 'making away with necessaries' and still more with either drunkenness and/or absence from parades. Rogers eschewed understatement when he remarked that they appeared to be 'a set of the most desperate villains and worthless thieves and vagabonds that ever disgraced any country in the world'. Heaven alone knew what the consequences would be if such men were ever left to their own initiative in the frontier region. But it was never put to the test. The governor appears to have quickly concluded that these men could not be trusted on any wider deployment.

Therefore it was only the scarcely more trustworthy RAC – their uniform comprising not so much the formal scarlet single-breasted coatee of popular imagination, but rather the more practical white linen jacket with blue facings, worn with white cotton trousers and black accoutrements (and in theory with the addition of a large cloak and a pair of flannel vests, though these were no doubt among the necessaries certain soldiers had been all too eager to hawk for ready cash) – which was ordered to the eastern frontier as intended, not so much to reinforce troop numbers there but rather, to Somerset's dismay, as replacement regular troops. But why were such troops needed and what were they expected to achieve?[3]

Defending the eastern frontier

The immediate difficulty stemmed from the fact that in the wake of the 1811–1812 Cape frontier war it was proving next to impossible to attract settlers to the newly administered Zuurveld region. Believing organised settlement to be the best – ultimately, perhaps, by means of affording its own protection, the only long-term guarantee of limiting continued Xhosa depredations and maintaining regional stability, Somerset had become focused on this issue. Already he had offered to remit the rent of potential settlers (at the time, of course, predominantly Boer settlers) for 10 years; in addition he was willing to grant a title in perpetual quit-rent after three years' occupancy. But no inducement seemed sufficient. Consequently, as Eric Walker put it, 'the anomaly of an expensive garrison guarding an almost empty country persisted'.[4]

That such a situation would in the ordinary course of events prove unacceptable to London was obvious, but how much more so in the worsening period of economic contraction, retrenchment, and social and political unrest consequent upon the ending of the Napoleonic wars. The necessity for economies had already been set out in a series of communications from Lord Bathurst, and it cannot have come altogether as a surprise when this began

---

3   Maclennan, *Proper Degree of Terror*, pp.174–175; Chartrand, *Émigré and Foreign Troops*, p.37.
4   E.A. Walker (ed.), *The Cambridge History of the British Empire, Vol. VIII: South Africa, Rhodesia and the High Commission Territories* (Cambridge: Cambridge University Press, second edition, 1963), p.219.

to impact on troop levels. The paradox was that it was these same social and economic conditions that lay behind developing plans for the prearranged settlement in the region of organised parties of what were called the United Kingdom's 'surplus population' (a Malthusian designation that particularly outraged William Cobbett – who himself would nonetheless have made an outstanding settler – and, to Somerset's undoubted discomfort, settler representative). Thus far-reaching changes were even now in the balance.

However, it was not simply the question of troop numbers that concerned and frustrated Somerset, important though that was: it was still more the quality. Somerset had taken the first opportunity to apprise Lord Bathurst of his concerns. He had adjudged the minimum number of troops necessary to defend the Cape Colony from either invasion or incursion to be some 4,000, but the number London arrived at was 2,400. That was bad enough. But Somerset had, as he put it (21 June 1817), at least 'calculated upon having … men upon whom dependence can be placed'. Instead he found himself placed in an almost impossible situation. 'The service of the frontier', he contended, 'cannot be carried on [with] under 1,100 men' [sic] and 'upon this service', he was adamant, 'I cannot employ the description of soldier [of] which the 60th regiment is composed.' What he called 'the ground of that Corps' consisted of 'foreigners, deserters, from all nations, grumblers, and of a general and desperate character'. Already, as if to underline the point, a section of the 60th posted to Robben Island for guard duties had taken the opportunity to seize a trading vessel and make good their escape. Yet consider the frontier environment into which such men were ultimately to be deployed. 'Desertion, there so easy, would', he pointed out, 'carry with it the greatest evils.'

Somerset therefore urged Bathurst to have the corps removed, lest deserters combine with elements of the Xhosa 'to lay the foundation of a predatory government' beyond colonial control. Perhaps he was recalling how the Boer Slagter's Nek rebels had forlornly attempted to forge an anti-British alliance with Ngqika – a fact that contributed towards Somerset's disinclination to grant the ringleaders clemency.

But if the deployment of such units were likely to be inimical to the maintenance of stability, what was the right calibre of troops for frontier service? Somerset was no fool in such matters. As governor he had always taken a close and intelligent interest in military affairs, and his defence plans had, with good reason, laid emphasis on the employment of dragoons. Indeed they constituted what he called the 'mainspring' of his system of frontier defence. Somerset's estimate of troop numbers to defend the Cape Colony had always included a cavalry element detailed for frontier service. That was precisely the element now to be denied him – to be replaced with a penal corps.[5]

It is therefore not difficult to imagine the depth of his frustration when he first learnt that the 21st Light Dragoons and the 83rd Foot were to be withdrawn for service in India and Ceylon. In one sweep a total garrison of 4,300 was to be reduced by some 1,500, and to consist almost solely of infantry.

---

5 A.K. Millar, *Plantagenet in South Africa: Lord Charles Somerset* (Cape Town: Oxford University Press, 1965), pp.102–103.

The 83rd had been part of the force that under Sir David Baird had recaptured the Cape in 1806. Extended service on the frontier was never without its attendant disciplinary problems, but the regiment had gained 11 years' valuable experience in the colony.

The Cape Regiment was also to be disbanded, although its creation and deployment had proved a notable success, which even today is inadequately remembered. As Johan de Villiers observed, the soldiers 'proved to be accurate shots and reliable in every respect'. 'Not one of them', he noted, 'deserted during the arduous operations in which the Xhosa … were driven from the Zuurveld.'[6] Indeed, after the war the regiment was enlarged to 800 soldiers, an increase in expenditure, with Major Thomas Lyster succeeding Graham, who left the frontier in June 1812. Major George Fraser then, in turn, succeeded Lyster in 1815, having, in the course of his duties, to attend to the Slachtersnek affair.

However, by 1816 financial constraints were not to be circumvented even in this case. The regiment was officially disbanded on 24 September 1817, to be replaced by a small force that included a troop of dragoons and was entitled the 'Cape Corps of Infantry and Cavalry' or the 'Cape Light Infantry and Cape Cavalry'.[7] Raised for the defence of the eastern frontier, the new unit was nowhere near adequate for the task, as was soon apparent, and this retrenchment was resented and remembered within the service. 'The want of the old Cape Corps [sic], with its discarded officers, was then very much felt', Stockenström noted in relation to the events of 1818/19, 'and excited a great deal of acrimony and scandal.'[8]

The rag tail RAC units dispersed among the frontier posts did not compare, being to all appearances dangerously untrustworthy. Again theft and a propensity to violence (even among themselves) seemed to be endemic; but more shocking still was when in October 1817 six men deserted along the Fish River, at least three of whom were known to have stolen guns and to have murdered a canteen keeper on the Swartkops before being apprehended.

The governor could barely contain his anger. It is something of a commonplace to cite the Duke of Wellington's remark about soldiers generally being 'the scum of the earth', but in this case it appeared all too evidently true. Somerset went so far as to report that the new troops had occasioned 'such terror in the interior' that 'so far from being able to persuade settlers to repair to those fertile districts, even those who remained are taking measures for abandoning a country where their lives and property are in imminent danger from those who have been placed there for their protection'. This sounds exaggerated, and no doubt there was a political point to be made, but that Somerset both objected to and continued to distrust the corps is beyond question.[9]

---

6 J. de Villiers, *Die Cape Regiment, 1806–1817*, p.238.
7 Tylden, *Armed Forces of South Africa*, p.57; J. de Villiers, *Die Cape Regiment, 1806–1817*, p.238.
8 Hutton (ed.), *Stockenström*, I, p.117.
9 Maclennan, *Proper Degree of Terror*, pp.174–176.

Persistent frontier problems and RAC acclimatisation

Somerset had reason to be angry, but the situation should not be viewed out of context. As Somerset had effectively acknowledged, a wide range of problems already existed. Thus the deployment of the RAC will at most have exacerbated an already difficult situation. Not only were there a lack of appropriate settlements and an undermining of Somerset's defence plans but, as seen, desertions had also always been – and would, indeed, remain – an important and seldom examined subtext to the British army's long involvement both along the Cape frontier and beyond it.

What Somerset did not anticipate was that the RAC rank and file might eventually start to moderate their behaviour and, under the authority of good officers, become commendable soldiers. But that was the purpose of the harsh discipline that Wellington endorsed; that had happened in the past and that is indeed what happened again, up to a point.

Beginning with John Fraser himself, the corps had throughout its service contained some surprisingly good officers. Probably the best known was the Irish-born French émigré and dedicated abolitionist, Charles MacCarthy, who as governor of Freetown, Sierra Leone, would subsequently (in 1824) lead an expedition against the Ashanti, which would end with his heart being eaten by the Ashanti chiefs and his head being used as a trophy on state occasions. But more instructive, perhaps, was the corps' rather more tenuous association with John Gurwood.

Gurwood was later to become one of Wellington's private secretaries and the celebrated editor of the duke's *Dispatches*, but at one stage he briefly held a commission in the RAC. This was because promotions as a result of gallantry in the field (as opposed to by purchase) would often be redeemed in a regiment where commissions were less competitive. Thus Gurwood was a lieutenant in the 52nd Foot – part of the first Corps of Light Infantry formed under Sir John Moore, and one of the elite regiments of the Peninsular War – when he led the Light Division's Forlorn Hope of 25 men in the attack on Ciudad Rodrigo in January 1812; but being such a junior officer (listed as thirty-third lieutenant: the future governor of the Cape, George Napier, was one of his senior officers), he was awarded a captaincy in the RAC.

The appointment is likely to have owed something to the fact that the corps had a colonel with no small influence at the Horse Guards in Whitehall: General (Sir) James Willoughby Gordon. Gordon had seen service in the West Indies before becoming successively Military Secretary to the Commander in Chief 1804–1809, Commissary in Chief to the Forces 1809–1812, Quartermaster General in the Peninsular theatre from August to December 1812, and Quartermaster General to the Forces from 1813 until his death in 1851. In this last role in particular he worked closely with Lord Charles Somerset's younger brother, the Military Secretary Lord FitzRoy Somerset (the future Lord Raglan, Commander in Chief in the Crimean War). But Gordon also served as lieutenant colonel, colonel commandant, and colonel of the RAC from 1808 to 1815, in the latter stages of the Napoleonic wars (a regiment, one should note, would generally have two lieutenant colonels, only one of whom would serve with the regiment at any given time, while the honorary colonelcy of a regiment would generally be offered to a senior officer who, while having no operational responsibilities, would then be expected to take an interest in regimental affairs and officer selection). And as even the highest-ranking staff officers were listed under their regimental affiliations, it was as Major General J.W. Gordon, Royal African Corps, that he was appointed quartermaster general.[10]

'The Blundering Commando'

Continued Xhosa raiding during the latter part of 1817 compelled the governor, Lord Charles Somerset, to institute measures to deal with the situation. Therefore the truncated and hastily assembled Cape Corps of Infantry and Cavalry, placed under the command of Lieutenant Colonel George Fraser, the last CO of the Cape Regiment, was almost immediately detailed to undertake a most ticklish task. On 5 December, Fraser was instructed to assemble a commando in order to obtain redress from the 'guilty party', 'without', as the directive had it, 'injuring or even molesting those kraals whose chiefs have evinced their rectitude by a faithful adherence to the treaties entered into with them'. The 'guilty party', Somerset made clear, was Ndlambe, and he was, if possible, to be captured and escorted back to the colony as a prisoner.[11]

Thus, on 8 January 1818, Fraser led a burgher commando together with a detachment of the new Cape Corps from Grahamstown and through Trompetter's Drift, heading for Ndlambe's Great Place, situated east of the Fish River near where Peddie would later be established. But Ndlambe was forewarned of the danger and had time to drive his cattle away from the vicinity. When Fraser got there, there were simply no cattle and consequently there was no means of obtaining redress – not, at least, from that source. Moreover, as Fraser conversed with Ndlambe, three divisions of Rharhabe Xhosa encircled the commando.

Fraser seemed both intimidated and confused as how best to proceed. 'As he [Ndlambe] had no inducement to offer any resistance to my party', he later explained, 'my orders did not empower me to seize his person.'[12] Instead, he went beyond Somerset's instructions and ventured north into Ngqika's territory, from where he sequestrated some 2,060 head of cattle from sub-chiefs such as Xasa, Gretta, and Habana, shooting those Xhosa who resisted.

To the colonial frontiersmen these chiefs were notorious plunderers – a view shared by Fraser, who had intelligence to substantiate the claim. But the move was still difficult to reconcile with Somerset's instructions and demonstrated a growing divide between Cape Town and Grahamstown. It

---

10 E. Longford, *Wellington: The Years of the Sword* (London: Weidenfeld & Nicolson, 1969), pp.321–322; Haythornthwaite, *The Armies of Wellington*, p.156; R. Holmes, *Redcoat: The British Soldier in the Age of Horse and Musket* (London: Harper Collins, 2001), pp.111, 148–150, 173.
11 Maclennan, *Proper Degree of Terror*, p.177.
12 Maclennan, *Proper Degree of Terror*, p.177.

also shattered the trust that the missionary Joseph Williams had rebuilt with the Xhosa in general and Ngqika in particular (it was never re-established: Williams died at the Kat River mission station in August 1818). Ngqika immediately protested that these chiefs were his adherents and that he had been betrayed by Somerset, an accusation the governor took seriously as potentially undermining his whole frontier policy.

Somerset therefore upbraided Fraser and issued instructions that Ngqika be compensated. However, given the time that had by then elapsed, this was anything but straightforward. Reputedly only 603 of the confiscated cattle were identified as stolen colonial livestock, but most of the remainder had already been distributed as compensation, so that a meagre 122 were all that were in the end returned.[13] Relations between Ngqika and Somerset survived the incident, but there were nonetheless unforeseen and unfortunate consequences.

The Battle of Amalinde

Ngqika was under pressure. He was being urged by his adherents to organise a campaign to recover the sequestrated cattle from the colony and could not be seen to rule it out if his diplomatic protests, as looked likely, yielded little. So he temporised. It was not enough. Xasa, Gretta and Habana and some other sub-chiefs transferred their allegiance to Ndlambe, who was unambiguously belligerent, needing only the right circumstances.

Following Ndlambe's expulsion from the Zuurveld in early 1812 the legendary figure of Nxele had emerged as a profoundly influential prophet in the ama-Ndlambe cause. Presently, as a result of Ngqika's evident weakness, which Fraser's 'Blundering Commando' (as it was later called) had exposed, and under Nxele's teaching (which Ndlambe was careful to cultivate), there emerged a powerful eastern Xhosa combination in opposition to Ngqika of the Rharhabe and the western Xhosa.

A drought in 1818 led to increasing disputes over grazing rights, with Ngqika allegedly appropriating grazing land belonging to Ndlambe and Hintsa, the Gcaleka paramount chief. However, Ndlambe was seeking to provoke Ngqika, and in this he was successful. By cattle raiding, this Ndlambe-led combination succeeded in drawing Ngqika's forces out of their strongholds in the Kat River and Tyume basins. It was October 1818.

The result was a devastating ambush in the Kommetjie flats at the Debe Nek, at the foot of the Intaba-ka-Ndoda (Ntaba kaNdoda) – an event known as the Battle of Amalinde. The clue to what must have occurred lies in these place names. *Amalinde* is a Xhosa word deriving, according to Professor Tim Couzens, from *indebe* meaning a ladle, just as *kommetjie* means 'small basin' in Afrikaans. In other words, Ngqika's forces were ambushed upon being lured by a decoy into undulating ground.[14]

---

13   Maclennan, *Proper Degree of Terror*, p.178; Mostert, *Frontiers*, pp.459–461.
14   T. Couzens, *Battles of South Africa* (Claremont, South Africa: David Philip, 2004), pp.67–70; DSAB I, p.588 (Ndlambe), p.597 (Nxele).

THE FIFTH CAPE FRONTIER WAR

Debe Nek, with Ntaba kaNdoda looming in the background. Site of the Battle of Amalinde, October 1818. (Cory, *Rise of South Africa* 1, 1910)

On 19 March 1827, the missionary W.J. Shrewsbury – of whom we shall hear more, but who, while awaiting permission from Hintsa to establish a mission station among the Gcaleka Xhosa, was based at the Wesleyville mission station, sited among the Gqunukhwebe Xhosa some 10 miles from the coast on the Twecu River – made a point of visiting the battlefield in the course of a visit to Ngqika. '[W]e were much interested in riding over what may be called the Waterloo of Kafferland', he wrote in his journal. It was 'a large plain full of holes or small pits, where a pitched battle was fought seven years ago [*sic*] between Hintsa and the subordinate chiefs Tslambi [Ndlambe], Dushani [Mdushane, son of Ndlambe] and Pato [Phatho, the son of Chungwa, the chief of the Gqunukhwebe tribe controversially killed in the course of the Fourth Frontier War], on the one side, and Gaika [Ngqika] and his subordinate chiefs on the other side'. Many, he was given to understand, had lost their lives. 'Hintsa was victorious and some hundreds of slain were left upon the field.'[15] 'The Kaffers make no prisoners unless it be a chief', he added, by way of extrapolation; and if not altogether true, it came close to being the case in this instance. An estimated 300 ama-Rharhabe died upon the battlefield, but the killing did not stop there. The event, it would appear, retained a degree of notoriety among the pan-Xhosa population.

---

15   H.H. Fast (ed.), *The Journal and Selected Letters of Rev. William J. Shrewsbury 1826–1835, First Missionary to the Transkei* (Johannesburg: The Graham's Town Series, Witwatersrand University Press, 1994), pp.50-51; DSAB II, pp.460–461: Mdushane (Dushane/Dushani).

47

CONTROLLING THE FRONTIER

WMS missionary, William James Shrewsbury, whose journal and letters constitute an important source both for the Battle of Amalinde and the 'Fetcani alarm'.

Shrewsbury was travelling on that occasion with 'Brother Shaw' (William Shaw, Director of the Wesleyan Methodist Missionary Society in southern Africa and the originator of the chain of mission stations beyond the eastern frontier) and was accompanied by two Gqunukhwebe Xhosa who had participated in the battle. ('It was singular', Shrewsbury commented in passing, 'that both ... men had fought against Gaika [Ngqika] under the Chief Pato [Phatho], and yet that they were now with us on a visit to Gaika to request him to send an embassy to ... Hintsa to persuade him to receive the Gospel.') On arrival, Shrewsbury noted, these men 'pointed out to us exactly the order in which the chiefs were arranged ... the heights above on which Gaika [Ngqika] was posted and the manner in which Hintsa in person conducted the attack up a very steep ascent through a thick wood, while the main body on both sides fought in the plain below'.[16]

Shrewsbury returned to the subject in more depth in a letter addressed to 'The Secretaries of the Wesleyan Missionary Society' at Hatton Garden in London on 31 March 1827 – that is some 12 days later. After explaining in more detail the delicate state of the organisation's relations with Hintsa and the purpose of the visit to Ngqika's 'residence' ('upward of 60 miles distant' from Wesleyville), he turned to his and Shaw's inspection of the site of what he again described as 'the Waterloo of Kafferland'.[17]

This event he again oddly misdated as 'only 7 years ago' – the statement, indeed, being underlined for emphasis. However, that would have made it after the Battle of Grahamstown, the date of which was a matter of record and which was, of course, contingent upon the Battle of Amalinde. But more pointedly, this time he also gave information as to the extent the two Xhosa who accompanied the missionaries over the battlefield had been armed for the ambush upon Ngqika's forces. 'It so happened that the two natives who accompanied us, had both fought in this engagement', he asserted, 'and having Fire-Arms, had done much execution.'[18]

---

16 Fast (ed.), *Shrewsbury*, p.51. The DSAB entry on Phatho records that he 'apparently ... did not take part' in the Battle of Amalinde: III, p.684 (entry by J.G. Pretorius). Shrewsbury's journal confirms that he did. For estimate of 300 ama-Rharhabe battlefield dead see Maclennan, *Proper Degree of Terror*, p.178, and Laband, *The Land Wars*, p.143.

17 School of Oriental and African Studies, Wesleyan Methodist Missionary Society (WMS), South Africa correspondence, MMS Box 301: Shrewsbury to Secretaries, Wesleyan Missionary Society, 31 March 1827.

18 WMS: MMS Box 301: Shrewsbury to Secretaries, Wesleyan Missionary Society, 31 March 1827.

Just how widespread (or skilfully operated) the use of firearms was in the course of the engagement must remain a matter of speculation, but that they were employed would seem a fact. Nor should it come as any surprise. Royal African Corps deserters along the frontier were, as seen, particularly notorious, Lieutenant Colonel Thomas Willshire later going so far as to blame them for revealing to the Xhosa the layout of the ground over which the latter intended to attack Grahamstown. But the problem did not lie with the RAC alone. Desertions were always an issue, and there was also the material influence of what were seen as rogue 'Dutch traders'. Moreover, in cattle raids firearms would specifically be sought and stolen.[19]

Also noteworthy is the emphasis Shrewsbury again laid upon Hintsa's personal participation in the battle, as described by the Xhosa guides.

> On yonder high mountain, above that Thicket – said they – Gaika [Ngqika] was posted with a numerous body of men; & up that hill, & through the Thicket, Hintsa led on the attack in person, & fought his way to Gaika's company. In the meantime Hintsa's confederates, Tslambi [Ndlambe], Dushani [Mdushane], & Pato [Phatho], were stationed here in the Plain. Gaika's [Chi? edge of page missing] descended from that other Mountain to the Left, & engaged [them?].[20]

This, of course, formulates the guides' description in Shrewsbury's words, but it was presumably more or less what Shaw heard as well.

But if Hintsa personally engaged in the fighting in this manner, the fact remains that the victory was principally Ndlambe's; Ndlambe's victorious army was not under the direct command of Hintsa, but rather of Ndlambe's son, Mdushane, who was clearly no mean tactician. Previously estranged from his father, reputedly by reason of the status accorded his mother, the reconciliation had profound consequences, as it was Mdushane who coordinated a strikingly successful ambush. Certainly Ngqika appears to have been, if not complacent, then at least unprepared for a trap conceived with such ingenuity and sprung with such proficiency. The warriors placed strategically in the plain to entice the ama-Rharhabe forward comprised the more inexperienced of the ama-Ndlambe forces. It was expected that they would give ground, while the more seasoned elements – supported by a Gcaleka contingent led by Hintsa in person – lay in wait in a nearby forest.

It is reputed to have been Ngqika's commander Manxoyi who actually led the ama-Rharhabe into the ambush, after which there was limited room for manoeuvre, most particularly from among the traditional Xhosa (in this case ama-Rharhabe) wings; but in reality, even Maqoma, Ngqika's 'right-hand son' (that is, born of Ngqika's right-hand house and thus ultimately not in line to succeed him), who was subsequently to become the outstanding Xhosa commander of the Cape Frontier Wars and who fought with characteristic courage, was beaten and compelled to flee the field.

---

19 W.K. Storey, *Guns, Race and Power in Colonial South Africa* (Cambridge: African Studies Series, Cambridge University Press, 2011), p.55.
20 WMS: MMS Box 301: Shrewsbury to Secretaries, Wesleyan Missionary Society, 31 March 1827.

Escape was no easy matter. The ama-Rharhabe had been encircled and were caught in a desperate fight for survival, which appears to have lasted for several hours before, as dusk approached, Maqoma's amaJingqi warriors – his trusted *amafanenkosi* or 'circumcision-mates' (his following becoming the Jingqi tribe) – finally broke free of their enemy and made for the arduous incline of the Intaba-ka-Ndoda, Maqoma having to be helped or carried from the field. They were, in other words, making for what Shrewsbury described as 'the heights above on which Gaika [Ngqika] was posted', climbing the 'very steep ascent' up which 'Hintsa in person conducted' an attack.[21]

It was, on the face of it, a stunning ama-Ndlambe triumph; but if victory 'in a true sense' is, as Liddell Hart states, to be measured in political results, or at least improved prospects, then the victory was a chimera. The battle was decisive in Xhosa history, but for the wrong reasons. War without any determined purpose is simply bloodshed, an end in itself. At Amalinde the killing went on unchecked, even after the central fighting was over: but unrestrained as it was (some of the wounded left on the battlefield are reputed to have been impaled) it was still insufficient. Ngqika and his eldest son, Maqoma, succeeded in escaping to the Winterberg, from where Ngqika appealed to Lord Somerset for help. Somerset was quick to respond.[22] A punitive expedition was dispatched against the ama-Ndlambe. The resistance it presently provoked would be inspired by an apocalyptic vision. A spark had been lit.

Brereton's commando against Ndlambe

Ndlambe sent the usual protestations of peace, but Somerset believed that his aim was to annul Ngqika's 'pacific system', and that the situation therefore demanded an immediate response.[23] The resultant expedition fell under the command of the new commandant of Grahamstown, Lieutenant Colonel Thomas Brereton.

Born in Ireland in 1782, Brereton had (save for a brief period in Jersey, from 1803 to 1804) served in the West Indies from 1798 to 1813, principally as an officer of the Royal West India Rangers. However 1814 saw his appointment as lieutenant governor of Senegal and Goree; and the following year he was gazetted lieutenant colonel, Royal African Corps.

Notwithstanding the ill repute of the corps, Brereton's appointment as commander of the eastern frontier can presumably be seen as some measure of confidence – in him, if not his former unit. Certainly, contrary to the impression one gains from most accounts, he was not without active military experience, having served as Major of Brigade to Major General Sir Charles Wade during the latter's sharply contested capture of Guadaloupe in 1810. But

---

21 DSAB II, pp.460–461; Laband, *The Land Wars*, pp.80, 142–144; Fast (ed.), *Shrewsbury*, p.51.
22 Mostert, *Frontiers*, pp.466–467; Laband, *The Land Wars*, p.143; B.H. Liddell Hart, *Thoughts on War* (London: Faber & Faber, 1944/repr. Staplehurst: Spellmount, 1999), pp.42–43; DSAB I, p.588 (Ndlambe), p.592 (Ngqika).
23 Maclennan, *Proper Degree of Terror*, p.178.

if it was a measure of confidence, then it was misplaced. Brereton's previous experience belied a temperamental flaw: as his later life would show, he was not at his best when under pressure. And pressure there certainly was, for he arrived at Grahamstown on 6 October 1818, at a time when tensions were high but intelligence was limited. Orders to lead a commando were received a mere three weeks later.

Brereton's actions, it was made clear (remembering Fraser's 'Blundering Commando'), were supposed to be strictly proportionate and political. Thus he was to act in 'strict good faith' with the Xhosa and, within limits, to punish Ndlambe – always bearing in mind that the object was 'the future tranquillity of the border'.[24]

Such directions no doubt sounded well and good when laid before Lord Bathurst in London, but to a small commando risking life and limb in the bush, and acting on incomplete intelligence, they were altogether more abstract. Moreover, there was really only one way to secure the future tranquillity of the border by Somerset's calculation, and that was to use the opportunity carefully and efficiently to drive the ama-Ndlambe beyond the Keiskamma River. But to achieve that aim with the desired economy of force even an experienced commando would have had to have been assembled in secrecy and then launched quickly, without warning. Brereton not only lacked such experience, but the slow mustering of his force in Grahamstown at a time of great tension could not be kept hidden, and its movements were compromised from the start.

That Ndlambe was well informed is obvious, not least because he had living with him a coterie of RAC deserters, one of whom, said to have been a sergeant of the line, had gained the status of a sub-chief.[25] This man would have had his own followers and have exercised his own intelligence network, in much the same way as other figures that will appear in the course of this narrative and, indeed, beyond it – the Boer Nicholas Lochenberg, the deserter Robert Joyce and even the early Natal settlers like John Cane and Henry Ogle come to mind. However, these others were active well beyond the volatile colonial frontier. The RAC deserters were not. Thus not without reason did Somerset fear the possible emergence of what he had called 'a predatory government' of warring Xhosa, disaffected Khoikhoi, army deserters and irreconcilable Boers if the situation were allowed to continue unchecked.

Nor were Brereton's initial efforts greatly helped by Andries Stockenström, who was at that time landdrost of Graaff-Reinet. Born in 1792, Stockenström had as early as 1808 acted as Dutch interpreter to Colonel Collins's expedition to the Orange River and into what was then called 'Kaffirland'; after which, in 1810, he had accompanied the commando sent to inform Ndlambe of the government's decision to expel him from the Zuurveld region. Thereafter, in January 1811, he gained a commission in the Cape Regiment, and as an ensign participated in the Fourth Cape Frontier War against Ndlambe. For a time Stockenström acted as his father's ADC, and then when his father

---

24 DSAB III, pp.104–105; Mostert, *Frontiers*, p.467.
25 Maclennan, *Proper Degree of Terror*, pp.189–190.

Andries Stockenström, 1792-1864, a portrait taken in middle age and subsequently used as the frontispiece of his autobiography

was killed he was appointed commander of the burgher force his father had been leading – and he afterwards, as seen, helped establish the settlement of Grahamstown.

An independently minded humanitarian, Andries Stockenström would come to play an increasingly important role on the eastern frontier over the following decades but, as was becoming apparent, he was as prone as the next man to personal animosities, which he hid behind an almost Gladstonian sense of his own rectitude. Thus he could at times come across as unwittingly patronising, and the brief critique of the Brereton commando given in his autobiography (made almost in passing) – temperate and justified as it may have been – carries an unfortunate sense of this. The Xhosa civil war had been about 'hunting grounds and other minor questions in which the Colony had no interest', he wrote somewhat unhelpfully; 'but our Government thought proper to espouse the cause of Gaika [Ngqika]', and so what he described as 'a powerful commando' was sent into 'Kaffir land'. Stockenström, with 'a Burger force', accompanied the commando 'to the heads of the Kat and Koonap Rivers … considering the eastern front of my district in danger', but in the event the force had, as he put it, 'little cause for fighting'.[26]

In reality, it was partly the need to await the arrival of the accompanying Boer commando that slowed down and compromised Brereton's expedition. Called out on 4 November, Stockenström initially demurred and arrived from Graaff-Reinet with an incomplete burgher force on 21 November.[27] It was 1 December 1818 before the 'powerful commando' set off. And a more than usually heterogeneous force it was, not so much as a result of the withdrawal of regular foot and cavalry – Brereton retained a detachment of 38th Foot – but rather through the unfortunate impact of the Treasury-lead disbandment of the Cape Regiment and its inadequate and resented replacement with the 'Cape Corps of Infantry and Cavalry'.

Nonetheless Brereton performed creditably, allowing for the fact that he had been placed in a most difficult and invidious position. Arriving at Ndlambe's Great Place on 7 December 1818, it was to find the area largely vacated. Ndlambe with his people and cattle had withdrawn to secluded bush valleys, in which conventional troops would be at a disadvantage. Taking no chances, Brereton therefore used his artillery as a means of dislodging them,

---

26   Hutton (ed.), *Stockenström*, I, pp.115–116.
27   Cory, *Rise of South Africa*, I, pp.376-377.

and in this he was initially successful. However, the commando having been reinforced by Ngqika's men, the operation then took a murderous turn. Far from simply dispersing Ndlambe's people and capturing cattle, they began slaughtering their adversaries until Brereton took the unprecedented step of temporarily disarming his allies.[28]

Ultimately, some 23,000 cattle were seized, 9,000 of which were given to Ngqika, while the remainder helped defray the cost of the expedition or compensated frontier farmers for alleged losses (Brereton's losses were remarkably slight: one man killed and one wounded). This did little to satisfy Ngqika, any more than the reinstatement of land to Ngqika was likely to quell the disaffection of the ama-Ndlambe. Consequently few (outside the colonial press) expected the outcome to be conducive to 'the future tranquillity of the border'. Brereton certainly did not, and warned of the need for the 'utmost vigilance'. So the frontier posts prepared for a period of containment. Intelligence reports highlighted the unease. 'We are without milk', said one ama-Ndlambe source, 'and the new king [Ngqika] will not give us any, so we must get some from the white man's king who has taken all our cattle and left us to perish.'[29]

Assertive raiding by the Xhosa began on Christmas day 1818 and became progressively more serious. On the night of 28 January 1819, Colonel Fraser's (the Cape Corps' commanding officer) own farm on the Kasouga River was raided and 85 cattle taken. On 31 January, Ensign Hunt of the RAC was killed, together with a private soldier, when their patrol was attacked at Upper Kaffir Drift. On 2 February, Captain Gethin of the 72nd Foot, together with a Sergeant Peacock and a Private Macdonald, lost their lives in an ambush near De Bruin's Drift.

That there should be no misunderstanding, Brereton, on 9 February, directed Fraser to ride back to Cape Town post-haste and advise Somerset personally of the rapidly deteriorating situation. It was, in reverse, the equal of Sir Harry Smith's celebrated Cape Town to Grahamstown ride of 1835, Fraser completing the some 600 mile distance in just over six days (arriving on 16 February 1819). However, Somerset was already aware of how things stood and needed no persuading to take action. Overcoming a little reluctance on the part of the ship's captain, he therefore directed the 18 gun frigate HMS *Favourite*, currently undergoing repairs in Simon's Bay, immediately to transport the light infantry of the 38th Regiment to Algoa Bay. However, when the ship's foremast was disabled, it had to return to dock and it was the end of the month before a transport ship, the *Alacrity*, was able to undertake the task.

In addition to the troops, the *Alacrity* carried additional supplies of wheat, flour, and other foodstuffs and a new commander to take over from Brereton, who had fallen out with Somerset. But perhaps most telling, in view of the recent unwelcome disbandment of the Cape Regiment and its replacement with a depleted Cape Corps of Infantry and Cavalry, was the inclusion of 150 stands of arms (a 'stand of arms' was a complete set of equipment for

---

28   Maclennan, *Proper Degree of Terror*, p.179.
29   Maclennan, *Proper Degree of Terror*, p.179; Mostert, *Frontiers*, p. 468.

CONTROLLING THE FRONTIER

'The Steerage of a Transport' on the Cape run: sketch by ensign R.H. Dingley, Cape Regiment. (Museum Africa, previously Africana Museum)

one soldier, that is, musket or rifle, bayonet, cartridge box or pouch and belt) with which Colonel Jacob Cuyler, the landdrost of Uitenhage, aimed to arm Khoikhoi for the defence of the region.[30]

Lieutenant Colonel Thomas Willshire assumes command of the frontier

On 22 January, before Fraser's ride, Brereton had written to Somerset's military secretary, Major George Rogers, advocating that a more covertly gathered and better-prepared force undertake a surprise attack against the ama-Ndlambe, who would then be driven 'quite over the Keiskamma'. However, just as he had done Fraser, in his frustration Somerset effectively upbraided Brereton, saying that he was supposed to have done that before, and to do so now only if he thought he could undertake the task properly this time. Brereton responded by tendering his resignation. He was placed in command of the garrison

---

30   Maclennan, *Proper Degree of Terror*, pp.180–182.

in Cape Town and returned to England in 1823. He later found himself in command of troops in Bristol at the time of the 1831 Reform riots, where, after losing control, he committed suicide rather than face a court martial.

It is difficult not to feel poor Brereton a little unjustly maligned, both at the time and subsequently. Noel Mostert is wrong to state that, just as in the Cape, Brereton 'became notorious for the brutality with which he put down rioters at Bristol'. The opposite is true, and it is perhaps an indication of political differences with a man like Somerset that after removing the 14th Light Dragoons from central Bristol in October 1831, he reportedly said to the crowd 'I'm for Reform, my boys, as well as you.'[31] It is a further irony that this should have occurred in Beaufort territory, although Lord Charles Somerset had died in February of that year.

Fortunately, Lieutenant Colonel Thomas Willshire of the 38th Foot was on hand as a replacement. The son of an army officer, Willshire had been born in Halifax, Nova Scotia, in 1789, and was 30 years old at this juncture. His father had purchased commissions for three sons in the 38th Foot when they were still children, so there was never much doubt as to their future, but it was 1807 before Thomas Willshire saw active service, first in South America and then, in the years following, during the Peninsular War. In 1812, he gained command of the Light Company of the 1st 38th (from 1771 a light company, comprising men selected for their character and marksmanship, was formally added to every regiment/battalion) and he was twice wounded in the course of Wellington's celebrated victory at Salamanca later that year. There followed a brevet lieutenant colonelcy, whilst within his regiment he gained the nickname 'Tiger Tom'.[32]

Deployed to the Cape Colony in June 1818 (landing on 2 November), the 38th had a fine reputation and in Lieutenant Colonel Thomas Willshire a most imposing commanding officer. What is more Bristol-born Charles Lennox Stretch, subsequently to become a controversial frontier figure strongly sympathetic to the Xhosa, was among his officers.[33]

The *Alacrity* arrived at Algoa Bay on 11 March 1819; however, although comprehensively briefed by the governor on the terms of the agreement with Ngqika and the forces that would be placed at his disposal, it was left to Willshire to decide whether it would be possible to cross the Fish River, take Ndlambe by surprise and drive him permanently beyond the Keiskamma. If, as Somerset suspected, it was not feasible, he should 'temporise', while retaining the authority to seize Ndlambe if the opportunity arose. In other words, Willshire was left essentially in the same position as both Fraser and Brereton before him. Would the outcome be any different?[34]

---

31 Mostert, *Frontiers*, p.469; G. Amey, *City Under Fire: The Bristol Riots and Aftermath* (Guildford: Lutterworth Press, 1979), p.54.
32 DSAB II, 849; Major W.J. Freer, *The Thirty-Eighth Regiment of Foot, Now The First Battalion of the South Staffordshire Regiment* (London: Harrison & Sons, 1916), p.294; C.R. Low, *Soldiers of the Victorian Age*, I (London: Chapman & Hall, 1880), pp.1–104.
33 B.A. le Cordeur (ed.), *The Journal of Charles Lennox Stretch* (Grahamstown: The Graham's Town Series, Maskew Miller Longman for Rhodes University, 1988), pp.2–3.
34 Millar, *Plantagenet in South Africa*, pp.115–116; Maclennan, *Proper Degree of Terror*, pp.183–184.

CONTROLLING THE FRONTIER

Cavalry of the Cape Corps. (Museum Africa, previously Africana Museum)

In one respect he was better served, for besides the reimposition of martial law, he had more Boers and troops at his disposal: 1,850 mounted armed burghers, 1,100 regular infantry, 32 Royal Artillery, 183 Khoikhoi cavalry from the Cape Corps of Infantry and Cavalry, and 150 Khoikhoi previously discharged from the late lamented Cape Regiment and now recalled for the ongoing emergency.[35] Characteristically, it was Willshire's intention to meet the problem head on, and 1 May was initially set as the date he would cross the Fish River into Xhosa territory. However, not only was such a build-up hardly conducive to a surprise attack, if that was the aim, the timetable had also to be delayed because insufficient fit horses could be collected in the continuing drought conditions after a bout of horse-sickness had spread throughout the frontier regions. Meanwhile, frustratingly, depredations increased.[36]

That the ama-Ndlambe might do more than simply raiding and dispersing in their accustomed manner was a danger specifically raised by Brereton, and he had (much to Somerset's irritation) advocated that the danger be pre-empted, a proposition Willshire supported. However, what the frontier forces failed to comprehend was the scale and, it might be said, ambition of the preparations beyond the Fish River. Ndlambe's military strength had not only remained unaffected by Brereton's 'powerful commando', but under the exhortations of the prophet Nxele, an attack was being planned the like of which had never before been experienced.

Nxele

The life of the Xhosa prophet, Nxele, has understandably generated much interest in post-apartheid South Africa, and it elicited no little interest at the time. His contemporary, the Scottish missionary, John Brownlee, subsequently investigated 'the origin and rise of the prophet Nxele'. Brownlee

---

35   Maclennan, *Proper Degree of Terror*, p.184.
36   Cory, *Rise of South Africa*, I, p.383.

had spent a brief period at Bethelsdorp, before resigning from the LMS on 1 November 1818 and being appointed missionary and government agent among the Xhosa – going to live near Ngqika in June 1820.[37]

Documentary evidence of Nxele's background is necessarily scant, but he was of poor Gonaqua lineage, born sometime in the late eighteenth century, and as a result of his father's inclination lived for a time at the Bethelsdorp mission station in the Uitenhage district, and also where the Wesleyville mission would subsequently be located. Even his name varies. *Nxele* means 'left' in Xhosa, indicating he was left-handed, but he was also known as Makanna, which appears to have been his original name, while the frontier Boers translated his name as *Links*(ch) (meaning left: that is, left-handed) – this in turn being rendered in English as Lynx.

However, we do know his father died when Nxele-Makanna was still young, after which his mother went to live among Ndlambe's people. As well as being withdrawn and given to periods of isolation in the wilderness, he must have been an unusually articulate and theologically educated young man, with a compelling presence. After his circumcision, he actually returned to the colony to spend some time in Grahamstown with the chaplain of the Cape Regiment. A.A. van der Lingen was moved by Nxele's evident sincerity and eagerness to learn, and therefore both welcomed and was favourably impressed by the young man.[38]

Thus, on returning to Ndlambe's people, Nxele appeared to be fired with more or less orthodox Christian zeal, and it was not welcomed. Indeed, he was eventually seized and taken before Ndlambe, and it was from that point that Ndlambe and Nxele coalesced. There emerged in no great time a formidable, culturally awakened, Xhosa confederation.

Precisely how these strands came together and intertwined is difficult to determine, but had Ndlambe not cultivated Nxele in the manner he did, it would never have come about. So what was it that Ndlambe saw in Nxele? The answer was not simply leadership of a culturally awakened Xhosa confederation, but the leadership of such a confederation in opposition to and at the expense of Ngqika.[39] Nxele soon acquired such a following that he was referred to in official Cape Colony correspondence as a chief. Intriguingly, in 1816, the LMS even contemplated establishing a mission station at his kraal. (In the end, as seen, Joseph Williams sited a mission on the Kat River, close to Ngqika.)

Nxele was clearly influenced by frontier missionaries such as Dr J.T. van der Kemp of Bethelsdorp, as well as A.A. van der Lingen – in particular by their teachings on the resurrection of the dead – and claimed both to be a brother of Christ and a prophet descended from the Xhosa creator, uHlanga. However, this theological synthesis became progressively more hostile to the

---

37 B. Holt, *Greatheart of the Border: A Life of John Brownlee* (King William's Town: The South African Missionary Museum, 1976), pp.14–18; DSAB I, pp.129, 598.
38 Maclennan, *Proper Degree of Terror*, pp.186–187. When the Cape Regiment was disbanded in September 1817, Van der Lingen left the service, returning to Holland the following year. He died in 1821.
39 Mostert, *Frontiers*, p.429.

whites with revelations about Mdalidephu, the God of the black man, and was presently to encompass the raising of Xhosa ancestors to help drive the whites out of the land.[40] After the Brereton commando, and with colonial forces preparing for a further incursion into Xhosa territory, the time had arrived for desperate measures.

So it was that Nxele made ready to lead the ama-Ndlambe confederation against the colony. Naturally Ngqika would have no part in the attack, but some of Hintsa's subordinate chiefs were induced to join what had taken on the aspect of a Xhosa jihad.

The Battle of Grahamstown

Ngqika's interpreter, Hendrik Nquka, was also involved. As an emissary, he was permitted to come and go from Grahamstown at will and was therefore well placed to spread disinformation. On 19 April 1819 he guilefully informed Willshire of developments beyond the Fish River (of which Willshire would have had a certain amount of intelligence), carefully insinuating that there was activity around Kaffir Drift, near the mouth of the Fish River. Willshire took the bait. Most of the light company of the 38th Foot was moved to the area, where doubtless there was indeed some diversionary activity.[41]

This reduced the garrison at Grahamstown by some 150 troops. Approximately 15 miles to the north-east, in the Fish River valley, were amassed some 6,000 Xhosa. The Royal African Corps' period of service in the Cape was about to culminate in one of the most dramatic confrontations in the history of the eastern frontier.

The incongruous, ritualistic start of the encounter seldom fails to bring one up short when reading about it. On 21 April 1819, an emissary arrived in Grahamstown with a message for Willshire: Nxele and Mdushane, the recent victor of Amalinde, would breakfast with him next morning. It was a declaration of war. Willshire answered gamely that they would find all in readiness for their arrival, but took no particular precautions, perhaps imagining the communication to be misinformation or simple bravado (psychological warfare as we might call it today) rather than genuine notice of a direct attack on Grahamstown.

The following morning, 22 April, Willshire was inspecting a mounted troop from the Cape Corps of Infantry and Cavalry some 12 miles to the east of Grahamstown, in the direction of Botha's Hill – 'near the wood to the east of Botha's abandoned place (about 12 miles distant from this to the left of the waggon-road leading towards Trompetter's Drift)', as the absent Fraser later described it in a letter to Colonel John Graham[42] – when, at about 10:30

---

40   J.B. Peires, *The Dead Will Arise: Nongqawuse and the Great Xhosa Cattle-Killing Movement of 1856–7* (Bloomington: Indiana University Press, 1989), pp.1–2; DSAB I, pp.596–598.
41   Maclennan, *Proper Degree of Terror*, p.190.
42   23 April 1819: published, slightly amended, in Cory, *Rise of South Africa*, I, p.391. For full text see Fraser to Graham, 23 Apr. 1819: C.T. Atkinson (ed.), *Manuscripts of Robert Graham Esq. of Fintry*, p.139. Note also Cory I, pp.385–386.

The Fish River, onetime eastern boundary of the Cape Colony

a.m., a report came in of a party of Xhosa raiding the Corps' cattle some half a mile away.

One might, in retrospect, argue that this was an obvious ploy and that a pursuit should perhaps have been eschewed, but Willshire was certainly not headstrong in his response, demonstrating both a care for the Cape Corps' Khoikhoi troopers, who would be adversely affected by the stock-theft, and a wider awareness. 'I am sorry to add', as Fraser subsequently wrote to Graham (who will have understood), 'that they [the Xhosa] succeeded in taking about a thousand head of cattle … most … belonging to the men of the Cape Corps, being the produce of their hard earnings for many years and the chief support of their women and children'.[43]

---

43   Published, slightly amended, in Cory, *Rise of South Africa*, I, p.391. For full text see Fraser to Graham, 23 Apr. 1819: C.T. Atkinson (ed.), *Manuscripts of Robert Graham Esq. of Fintry*, p.140.

According to the poet, journalist and philanthropist, Thomas Pringle, Captain William Harding was with Willshire at this time. Harding was an experienced officer, originally of the 20th Foot (with whom he had seen much service), who had transferred to the Cape Regiment as captain in 1812. Retiring from the service later in 1819, he became an important frontier official and friend of Pringle – to whom he related the particulars of these events.[44]

With 25 troopers Willshire gave chase towards Botha's Hill, but as they approached the ridge some 300 Xhosa were seen near the top in two distinct factions. It was the first intimation that something was amiss, and Willshire felt it. After crossing the spruit at the base and beginning to climb, Willshire noticed the Xhosa move back over the ridge. It had all the hallmarks of a trap; therefore, he slowed his steed, Blucher, and ordered two men back, to gain a better perspective. He then continued to climb, and sure enough out of sight of the main body of horsemen the Xhosa were seen to move down the flanks in an encircling manoeuvre.

Alerted to the danger, the men recrossed the spruit: but it was only the beginning. 'I was surprised to find', as Willshire later stated (with unconscious understatement), that 'we were followed by about five thousand [Xhosa], who gave a horrid yell, rushed down and crossed the river after us'.[45] The mounted troop made several attempts to check the Xhosa advance while word was sent back to the garrison, but they were merely buying time. By 11:45 a.m. the troop was back in Grahamstown and Xhosa warriors could be seen amassing on the hills overlooking the settlement.

There was then a short stand-off as the ama-Ndlambe Xhosa gathered. By 1:30 p.m. there were not only an estimated 6,000 warriors in place, armed with shields and assegais, smeared with red ochre and 'decorated round their elbows and knees with fringes … of ox-tails',[46] but also thousands of women and children with domestic accoutrements such as mats and pots, in anticipation of the white men being driven into the sea. In what might be described as a form of Xhosa millenarianism, Nxele had invoked their ancestors and declared that the bullets of their enemies would turn to water ('it was evident that they did not entertain a doubt of success', Fraser reported to Colonel Graham, 'otherwise they never would have attempted the like in open daylight and fine fair weather').[47]

Willshire and his second-in-command, Captain Charles Trappes, used this hiatus to their advantage, preparing defences and positioning the limited force at their disposal. Trappes was an experienced and able officer, who proved to be particularly effective at this moment of crisis. Born in 1776, he was initially commissioned in the 5th Foot and fought at Corunna before transferring to the 72nd later in 1809. In the course

---

44 Pringle, *Narrative*, pp.282, 343.
45 Maclennan, *Proper Degree of Terror*, pp.190–191.
46 Cory, *Rise of South Africa*, I, p.386. Mostert, *Frontiers*, p.475.
47 'From all I can learn I judge that the strength of the Kaffers … would have been about 5,000, though many who were present think there were at least from 8 to 10,000': Major G.S. Fraser to Colonel John Graham, 23 Apr. 1819, C.T. Atkinson (ed.), *Manuscripts of Robert Graham Esq. of Fintry*, p.139.

of the Peninsular War he then served as a lieutenant colonel of the 2nd Caçadores, a Portuguese light infantry regiment led in part by British officers, resulting from Major General William Beresford's reform of the Portuguese army (those officers who volunteered for service with the Portuguese in this way received an automatic step-up in rank. There were some 300 such officers over the course of the war). Coming to the Cape Colony with the 72nd in 1818, the regiment proceeded to the eastern frontier, where Trappes was appointed a worthy second-in-command to Willshire.[48]

The defenders comprised some 350 men: 45 soldiers of the 38th, 135 men of the RAC, 32 armed burghers ('probably the whole of the civilian male population of Grahamstown at that date', as George Cory reflected), a few artillerymen, and lastly 82 infantrymen and 39 troopers/cavalry of the Cape Corps of Infantry and Cavalry – most of the latter of whom had, with Willshire, not long regained the safety of the garrison town.[49]

Grahamstown at that time, Cory observed in 1910, 'had not made any great strides in its development'. The few houses 'gave no more than a suspicion that a street, the present High Street, was in course of formation'. 'The simple architecture of the buildings, standing upon the rough grass veldt' gave every 'appearance of a village community in its most primitive form'.[50] This primitive settlement lay surrounded by hills and bisected on the eastern side by a straggling spruit, the banks of which provided a defensive feature. Therefore Willshire and Trappes formed a line of defence along its path.

The southern end of the line, where Trappes was situated, fixed onto the barracks, with rising ground behind. One officer (Lieutenant Cartwright) and 60 men manned the barracks. At the northern end, meanwhile, Lieutenant Aitchison was directed to place two artillery pieces on a rise of land situated on the eastern side of the spruit, with a detachment of the RAC in support. This site ('near where the railway station now stands', as Cory tell us) commanded the slopes and flats across which the Xhosa were expected to attack. The cavalry troop and the remainder of the 38th Light Company was then placed below and slightly forward of these guns.

In addition, Willshire placed five guns west of the spruit, in front of the north end of the settlement, to cover his force's retreat if necessity arose. The infantry element of the Cape Corps was also positioned there as a reserve, lest an attack come in from an unexpected quarter.[51]

The Xhosa evidently knew the layout of the ground over which they intended to attack. Willshire was likely correct in his contention that their strategy had been delineated by 'some of those villainous deserters from the RAC'; but Xhosa intelligence was in any event good, knowing both how ill-defended the settlement was and from where likely reinforcements would have to come. Ngqika's aforementioned interpreter, Nquka, is most

---

48   He was a better soldier than administrator, as demonstrated when he was subsequently appointed provisional magistrate of the 1820 Settler township of Bathurst: DSAB II, p.748.
49   Cory, *Rise of South Africa*, I, p.388; Maclennan, *Proper Degree of Terror*, p.192.
50   Cory, *Rise of South Africa*, I, p.386.
51   Maclennan, *Proper Degree of Terror*, pp.192–193.

CONTROLLING THE FRONTIER

Grahamstown: watercolour attributed to 'an officer' after the Fifth Frontier War, Graham's tree still visible centre left, and post-war Drostdy House far right. Cory reproduced these images and dated them 1824. Certainly there is no church, which was begun that year. The drostdy was left unfinished in 1823, being one of Retief's unfulfilled contracts, precipitating his bankruptcy.

THE FIFTH CAPE FRONTIER WAR

Spruit on the eastern side of Grahamstown, with barracks to the left, scene of the fiercest fighting in 1819. (Cory, *Rise of South Africa* 1, 1910)

often mentioned as a spy in this respect. However the fact is that, largely as a result of Somerset's continuing policy of treating Ngqika as if he was the paramount chief of the Xhosa and investing him with undue authority, spies had effectively been invited into the heart of the frontier defences for years.

Fraser made specific reference to this in his 23 April letter to Graham: 'Previous to Colonel Brereton entering Kaffirland', he noted, 'Gaika sent (at my request) Hendrik Nootka and six others for the purpose of interpreting and conducting the commandos, etc., one of the six and Nootka was with me wherever I went in Kaffirland, that one named Stephanos and another of the six alluded to are also recognised among the dead'. 'It did not', he added, 'want that proof to convince me that no faith could be placed in those calling themselves Gaika's people'.[52] And indeed it did not, for as seen the so-called 'Blundering Commando' had already demonstrated the growing divide between Cape Town and Grahamstown regarding the nature and reliability of Ngqika's ostensible adherents.

From the situation that presented itself to Willshire, the Xhosa seemed intent on forming three divisions, two of which (comprising some 5,000 men) were to advance on the settlement directly, while the third (comprising 1,000 men) moved against the barracks. The aim, Willshire believed, was to 'turn my right and get into Grahamstown while I was engaged with their right and centre masses'. And having prepared to meet this stratagem, he moved a skirmishing line forward (for which the 38th Light Company was, of course, specifically adapted) in an effort to provoke the Xhosa into coming within range of his artillery.

---

52   Published in Cory, *Rise of South Africa*, I, p.391.

The Xhosa did come on, but not as Willshire anticipated. The smaller, third division of their force moved first, led by Nxele in person, and only after they began to engage the troops defending the barracks did the Xhosa right and centre 'set up a terrible yell' and charge on mass. It was, noted Willshire, 'a short distance in masses' and they then 'spread into clouds, covering the face of the hill'.

Perceiving from a vantage point on the west bank that the Xhosa were advancing beyond the right flank of the 38th, Willshire ordered the RAC detachment supporting the forward artillery to move right and plug the gap. Acting swiftly, they 'opened up a well-directed fire', Willshire noted, 'and completely stopped the Kaffirs from proceeding'. The guns were also well served, the six pounders issuing grape and canister to great effect. However, after initially recoiling, the Xhosa came on again to the very muzzles of the guns, the vanguard breaking their assegais to make use of them as close-combat stabbing (as opposed to throwing) spears.

This practice elicited particular comment from Thomas Pringle. It was a consequence of Nxele/Makanna's 'directions' to 'decide the battle in close combat', he observed. But whether the adoption of the stabbing spear in this way can be ascribed to Nxele directly is another matter. It would seem to have been an instinctive or intuitive response to the emergence of close-order combat, and as such had probably already been adopted in the course of the Battle of Amalinde just months before. And of course it was at about this time that Shaka was reputedly devising a system of fighting based on a similar weapon. Nonetheless, it was not something the colonial forces were used to. 'This was very different from [the Xhosa's] usual mode of bush-fighting', Pringle noted, 'but the suggestion of it evinces [Nxele's] judgment; for if promptly and boldly acted upon, it could not have failed of success.'[53]

To gain immunity from the white man's evil, Nxele had instructed the warriors to invoke the name of Tayi, son of Mdalidephu, and the name was shouted as they temporarily drove the gunners back. But they were unable to upturn or disable the guns before the position was regained, and from then on the line held. Instead of coming on again, the Xhosa formed their own irregular line at anything from 35 to 100 yards distance, where they knelt and crouched in the face of a continuing fire (both artillery and small arms) to which they were unable effectively to respond. Indeed, Willshire observed that they had a 'fear of looking at the fire' and on seeing a flash would immediately place 'the left arm with the kaross before their eyes'. Others, Fraser noted, 'leaped into the deep pools of water' and endeavoured to conceal themselves with grass and weeds. It was, Fraser wrote after the battle, 'really singular how few assegais were thrown' by the Xhosa, 'even when advanced close to the troops'. Most of them 'did not, as usual, carry one in the right hand', he noted, 'but kept them tied up together, in which state

---

53 Pringle, *Narrative*, p.282. 'There is no point in which popular writing about Shaka is so filled with romantic nonsense as on the issue of the long-bladed, short stabbing *umkonto*': Etherington, *Great Treks*, p.104fn.45.

THE FIFTH CAPE FRONTIER WAR

many bundles were taken out of the hands of the Kaffirs shot, without their having taken an assegai out'.[54]

Indirectly, there exists Xhosa testimony as to what it was like to be on the receiving end of this close and well-directed fusillade. One of the Rev. W.J. Shrewsbury's four converts when he established the new mission station of Butterworth in 1827/8 was a veteran both of the Battle of Amalinde and the attack on Grahamstown. This 'John Patross', as Shrewsbury christened him, may indeed have been one of the unnamed Xhosa who, as seen, had previously directed him and Shaw over the Amalinde battlefield. Writing on 30 June 1828, Shrewsbury provided his 'brethren' with a 'short account' of these converts and described Patross as being 'about 40 years of age' and as having had a 'very eventful' life. Wounded in the course of 'the memorable Battle fought between the Chiefs Gaika and Hintsa' (that is, Amalinde), he had been effectively left for dead there when 'a stout, hale Kafir, belonging to Gaika' noticed that he was still alive and 'resolved to dispatch him' – only for Patross to find the strength to overpower his adversary and escape to the bush. Then in the attack on Grahamstown he was again to the fore. 'The [defending] Infantry being commanded to return within the Trenches, that the Cannon might play upon the Enemy, so furious were the Kafirs, that many of them', as Shrewsbury wrote, 'rushed into the Trenches with the British soldiers, and the whole mass of them ran up to the very mouth of the Cannon [sic].' 'The Cannon, opening with Grapeshot just at that momentous crisis, produced a dreadful carnage, and the Caffres', Shrewsbury continued, 'began to retire in great consternation.' Patross was among them.

Xhosa warrior, lithograph, frontispiece from T.J. Lucas, *Pen and Pencil Reminiscences of a Campaign in South Africa* (London: Day & Son, 1861). Note bundle of assegais and kaross, both carried in left hand.

Shrewsbury then described Patross's direct experience. He retreated 'some distance, with several others', and with 'the Shot falling in every direction, they attempted to conceal themselves behind every Bush, or little mound of Earth that was near'. 'John', Shrewsbury wrote, 'stooped down behind an ant-heap, and while in this precarious situation, several times the Shot fell so near him that the Dust they raised [sic] was blown in his face.' That he survived to embrace Christianity was attributed to God.[55]

---

54   Maclennan, *Proper Degree of Terror*, pp.193–194; Fraser's letter to Colonel John Graham, 23 Apr. 1819: published (slightly amended) in Cory, *Rise of South Africa*, I, p.391. For full text see Fraser to Graham, 23 Apr. 1819: C.T. Atkinson (ed.), *Manuscripts of Robert Graham Esq. of Fintry*, p.139.
55   WMS: MMS Box 301, 18: Shrewsbury to 'Honoured Father and Brethren', 30 June 1828. In publishing this letter, Fast discreetly tidies Shrewsbury's punctuation and use of capitals: Fast (ed.), *Shrewsbury*, pp.XVI and 79. I quote from the original MS, because it conveys how Shrewsbury evidently wrote quickly and (as shall become apparent) under some pressure.

The third division moving against the barracks fared better. The Xhosa were in possession of the barrack square and, amid scenes of fierce fighting, forced an entry into the hospital, again employing short stabbing assegais.[56] It was at that point that Elizabeth Salt, the wife of the British soldier Sergeant Salt, reputedly aided the defenders – according to folklore smuggling a keg of gunpowder into the barracks disguised as a baby she was cradling (trusting to the supposed Xhosa custom of sparing women and children).

Born in southern France with the maiden name Covare, Elizabeth Salt was known as an itinerant wagon-shopkeeper, which suggests she was a hardy woman. But it is the fact that she was officially rewarded that confirms that she must indeed have played some role in these events. As to her actions, on her death in 1850 an obituary notice in the *Grahamstown Journal* stated that when the soldiers were on the point of retreating before 'overwhelming numbers', 'it was Elizabeth Salt that rallied and cheered them on to the fight, and served them with ammunition during the remainder of the engagement'.[57]

If she did aid the troops in this way it was a commendable act for an army wife, but unlikely to have been a decisive factor. Willshire, monitoring the battlefield as a whole, was aware of the situation and, doubtless at Trappes's instigation, moved the Cape Corps reserve up in support. The Xhosa were driven out. No less than 102 Xhosa dead were later counted within the confines of the barracks.[58]

Support also came with the fortuitous arrival of a party of 130 buffalo hunters under their Khoikhoi chief, Boesak. Jan Boesak was a Christian convert from the 'Hottentot' mission at Theopolis. His had not been an unequivocal path to Christ but, in contrast to Nxele, it finally rested upon conventional Christianity and, by extension, the defence of the colony. So when they saw the crisis at hand, Boesak and his men immediately joined the garrison's defence of the settlement – to the cheers of the British and colonial troops. The 'old Hottentot Captain Boezak', according to Thomas Pringle, knew 'most of the Caffer chiefs and captains … personally', and was 'familiar with their fierce appearance and furious shouts'. Therefore '[s]ingling out the boldest of those who, now in advance, were encouraging their men to the final onset', Boesak and his followers ('among the best marksmen in the colony') 'levelled in a few seconds a number of the most distinguished chiefs and warriors'.[59]

The attack across a broad front having wavered, Willshire judged it the moment finally to drive the Xhosa from the field. On the advance, the Xhosa fell back and scattered. It looked like a rout, but Willshire was careful to keep matters in hand. As he related, the Xhosa took flight 'so excessively fast' that the troops were 'not long able to keep up'. Therefore, 'not wishing them to pursue too far I sounded the retreat, and brought the troops back to the place where the guns were'; 'lest', he explained, 'a body of [Xhosa] … take advantage of the troops being so far from their guns and the town, and make

---

56   Cory, *Rise of South Africa*, I, p.390.
57   DSAB I, p.684.
58   Maclennan, *Proper Degree of Terror*, p.195; Cory, *Rise of South Africa*, I, p.390.
59   Pringle, *Narrative*, p.283; Maclennan, *Proper Degree of Terror*, p.195.

a rush to get in their rear'. In a more conventional battle the cavalry might be expected to follow through, but as Thomas Pringle noted, 'the handful of [Cape Corps] cavalry durst not follow them into the broken ravines where [the Xhosa] precipitated their flight'.[60]

In reality the Xhosa were demoralised, exhausted and had lost all cohesion, but Willshire with the small force at his disposal was wise to be prudent. By 5:00 p.m. the battle was over, with only dead or wounded Xhosa remaining. Later that night a burgher commando arrived, helping to secure the town.

Casualties

The number of dead and wounded in the immediate vicinity of the fighting was not as great as might have been anticipated. Many of the wounded limped, crawled or had been carried off the field by their comrades. Those remaining will thus have been severely wounded, and if signs of life were subsequently evident, they were simply dispatched. Consequently many more will have died away from the battlefield. This explains to some extent the discrepancy in the estimates given for the number of Xhosa killed in the battle.

Willshire, in a letter to Stockenström written three days later, put the figure at just 150 – although as many as 700 or 800 assegais had been picked up in the immediate vicinity. However he acknowledged that the number of (missing) wounded 'were very great indeed', so that many others would have crept away or hidden in bushes, to die later. Similarly George Fraser, who had been away inspecting horses at frontier posts when the attack came and only returned the following day (and therefore presumably derived the figure from the same source), reported 147 Xhosa dead 'in the immediate neighbourhood'. This figure was to rise after there had been more time to evaluate the extent and consequences of the conflict. Not a month later, on 15 May 1819, the *Cape Town Gazette* was reporting as many as 500 Xhosa 'sacrificed to the temerity of their chiefs'.[61]

However, Thomas Pringle subsequently placed perhaps more a more balanced estimate in the public domain. 'The slaughter', he reported, 'was great for so brief a conflict. About fourteen hundred Caffer warriors strewed the field of battle; and many more perished of their wounds before they reached their own country.'[62] Did this figure come from his main source, Captain Harding? It is, on the face of it, a significant difference. But a lot may depend on what constitutes the 'field of battle': was it a reference, as before, to the defensive line positioned immediately east of Grahamstown itself, or something wider than that?

---

60 Maclennan, *Proper Degree of Terror*, p.195; Pringle, *Narrative*, p.283.
61 Maclennan, *Proper Degree of Terror*, p.197; Fraser to Graham, 23 Apr. and 1 May 1819: C.T. Atkinson (ed.), *Manuscripts of Robert Graham Esq. of Fintry*, pp.138–141.
62 Pringle, *Narrative*, p.283. Pringle's *Narrative of a Residence in South Africa*, although published in 1834, was intended for publication as early as 1825 and was thus written much earlier.

There is also perhaps evidence of a growing folk memory or element of legend surrounding this event – particularly after the arrival of the 1820 Settlers – giving rise to a certain amount of overstatement in the figures. Thus the nineteenth century historian of the Settlers, Colin Turing Campbell (1824–1897), could write of how 'about 2,000 Kafirs strewed the battlefield, while many perished of their wounds along and in the rivulet down to the East Barracks' – an exaggeration that not even Cory could swallow. 'A little under 1,000 is perhaps [nearer] the mark', he observed.[63]

The interpreter and spy, Hendrik Nquka, was among those killed on the battlefield, if not directly in combat. He was captured on Willshire's orders as the Xhosa were being driven from the field – for, to his surprise, Willshire actually encountered Nquka in the confusion. 'I must have passed him, as the man who took him called to me from behind, and was on the point of shooting him when I rescued him', he related – the term 'rescued' being used in a somewhat qualified sense, since he 'gave him in charge of a dragoon [presumably of the Cape Corps cavalry, and as such a term revealing of their role], intending to hang him when I had done with the Kaffirs'. But such demarcations in the midst of all the confusion, killing and anger that is a battle, with hundreds milling about in all directions, are difficult to maintain, and Willshire had no sooner turned away when a shot rang out behind. Ignoring remonstrations to the contrary, 'Mr Rafferty', saddler of the Cape Corps cavalry, had blown Nquka's brains out.[64]

Also killed were three 'minor sons' of Ndlambe and some other 'petty chiefs'. As for British and colonial casualties, Cory recorded that 'three white men were killed, one of whom was Captain Huntly of the Royal African Corps'; but the authority for this is uncertain (as he admitted) and reports of two men killed, one white and one Khoikhoi Cape Corps trooper, are probably more accurate. Fraser confirmed the deaths of the two Cape Corps troopers, but stated that a private of the RAC had also been killed, while in addition two RAC privates had been 'dangerously wounded' and two RAC sergeants and two privates 'slightly wounded'. In a separate incident, five soldiers of the RAC were killed elsewhere that day.[65]

Colonel Graham, by then commandant of Simon's Town and in deteriorating health, was less than charitable or fair in his condemnation of Willshire's handling of the situation – being particularly scathing of the utility of European troops. He gave every appearance of being resentful of outside

---

63   C.T. Campbell, *British South Africa: A History of the Colony of the Cape of Good Hope from its Conquest 1795 to the Settlement of Albany by the British Emigration of 1819, with notices of some of the British Settlers of 1820* (London & Cape Town: John Haddon & Co., 1897), p.25; Cory, *Rise of South Africa*, I, p.390. Campbell presumably took the figure from a poorly compiled account written many years later by C.L. Stretch, published in the *Cape Monthly Magazine* of May 1876 and reproduced in D.C.F. Moodie, *The History of the Battles and Adventures of the British, the Boers, and the Zulus, etc., in Southern Africa from the Time of Pharaoh Necho to 1880, with Copious Chronology*, vol. I (Cape Town: Murray & St. Leger, 1888/London: Frank Cass & Co., Cass Library of African Studies, facs. reproduction, London 1968), pp.196–199.

64   Maclennan, *Proper Degree of Terror*, pp.197–198.

65   Fraser to Graham, 23 Apr. 1819: C.T. Atkinson (ed.), *Manuscripts of Robert Graham Esq. of Fintry*, p.140; Cory, *Rise of South Africa*, I, p.390; Maclennan, *Proper Degree of Terror*, p.198.

interference in the administration of what he called 'my town', the defence of which, he made clear, would be better left to Boer commandos and regular Khoikhoi troops (thereby overlooking the difficult working relationship between these two groups, which he had previously highlighted).[66]

One can imagine Graham among those idiosyncratic, but remarkable officers active under Henry Lawrence in the Punjab some 30 years later. However, as far as Willshire was concerned, there was never any shortage of backbiting when it came to administering the eastern frontier; he had more pressing concerns.

Willshire seeks to take the offensive

There were further alarms over the following days and Willshire remained on the alert, but otherwise the shock was absorbed and preparations resumed for the delayed campaign, to be undertaken in Xhosa territory. For all the importunate advice and criticism to which he was subject, however, Willshire declined to act precipitately. Not only was the deleterious effect of the horse-sickness still causing particular difficulties, but also the various detachments of burghers were displaying a marked reluctance to serve on commando.

Nor would he launch the campaign until he was sure that his base had been rendered secure. As if to underline the point some 300 Xhosa attacked the post at the Upper Kaffir Drift on 8 May. If Willshire had moved headlong into Xhosa territory and left Grahamstown inadequately defended, a Xhosa attack would place the security of the whole frontier in danger. He therefore sought reinforcements from Cape Town.

Reinforcements, comprising men from the 38th and 54th Foot, duly arrived at Grahamstown on 28 June 1819. With them came Major William Holloway RE, who was to oversee the defences and fortifications of the region. Holloway had assisted in the design and construction of the celebrated Lines of Torres Vedras in Portugal (and, later in the Peninsular War, was severely wounded in the siege of Badajoz) before being sent to the Cape Colony as commander of the Royal Engineers in October 1818.[67] Willshire had estimated that it would take Holloway approximately a fortnight to secure Grahamstown's defences, but on inspection Holloway stated it would take a month, the posts along the Fish River having also to be strengthened. Thus the campaign finally commenced on 28 July 1819.

Willshire's force was divided into three columns. The right column, under an impatient and frustrated George Fraser, comprised 160 mounted men of the Cape Corps and 388 armed burghers on commando duty from George and Uitenhage; the centre column, under Major Abbey of the 72nd Foot, comprised 400 regular infantry, 68 Cape Corps cavalry, 400 mounted burghers from Swellendam, Stellenbosch and elsewhere, some Royal Engineers and 32 artillerymen, accompanying four field-pieces; while the

---

66 Graham to unspecified recipient, 16 Feb. 1820: C.T. Atkinson (ed.), *Manuscripts of Robert Graham Esq. of Fintry*, pp.143-145; Maclennan, *Proper Degree of Terror*, pp.89, 198–199.
67 Maclennan, *Proper Degree of Terror*, pp.200–203; DSAB II, p.320.

left column, under Stockenström, comprised 560 mounted burghers from Graaff-Reinet. In addition, a combined reserve of 360 armed burghers and regular troops was based in Grahamstown, from where they were distributed among the recently strengthened posts on the Fish River.[68]

Willshire accompanied the well-equipped central column. In contrast to the more mobile and lightly provisioned commandos that formed the outer columns, the artillery-supported central column carried in tow four ammunition carts, a forage cart, 59 provision wagons, entrenching tools, ammunition supplies and a (to Willshire unwelcome, but politically prescribed) ama-Rharhabe entourage consisting of Ngqika, his son Maqoma and some 600 warriors.

Crossing the Fish River on 29 July, the column proceeded in difficult conditions to the Kat River, which was also crossed after Major Holloway's engineers had constructed a temporary bridge in the driving rain; but it was slow, arduous, progress. The left column under Stockenström, meanwhile, moving down from the source of the Tyumie, reached Ndlambe's Great Place on 31 July. It appeared to be deserted and Stockenström was preparing to move on to the rendezvous point with Willshire, Funa's Kraal, when reports came back of large numbers of Xhosa secluded in the neighbouring bush. But by then torrential rain had made it impossible for the men to keep their powder dry and operate their firearms. Instead of attacking the Xhosa, the commando therefore encamped, fearful of being subjected to an attack itself.

The Xhosa appeared to be closing in under cover of darkness, and on the alarm being raised and with firearms still inoperable Stockenström prepared for close-order combat; but fortunately, Ndlambe either decided against attacking or he was merely masking the commando's camp while withdrawing his followers and livestock towards the Keiskamma. Thus by the time the three columns met up, with the appearance of Fraser's commando on 4 August, Ndlambe had fled. So Willshire began the task of clearing the area between the Fish and Keiskamma rivers (some 25 miles across), much as Graham had done with the Zuurveld nearly a decade before.[69]

For this task the two commando formations received reinforcements. A contingent of 240 burghers of the Swellendam commando, under its elderly commandant Jacobus Linde, joined Fraser, who had been directed to divide his force, with one detail pursuing Ndlambe, while the other deployed in front of the Fish River to prevent the ama-Ndlambe from doubling back into its dense bush and ravines. Meanwhile, starting from Funa's Kraal and moving down to the mouth of the Fish River, Stockenström's expanded commando was to comb the intermediate area for Xhosa.[70]

Stockenström undertook the task systematically: 'great numbers of them were shot', he admitted, 'and the extent of their distress was more than I

---

68 Maclennan, *Proper Degree of Terror*, p.204.
69 Maclennan, *Proper Degree of Terror*, pp.205–206. Mostert caricatures Willshire as a sort of prototype Colonel Blimp – with his setting out at the wettest time of year just one of his 'ludicrous' and 'ignorant' innovations: *Frontiers*, pp.481–482. There were, of course, many reasons for this state of affairs, not least the previous horse-sickness and the not unrelated reluctance of the burghers.
70 Maclennan, *Proper Degree of Terror*, p.206.

Boer commando, a sketch by coppersmith, engraver and pioneer Cape photographer, William Syme, 1824-1866. (Museum Africa, previously Africana Museum)

can describe'. But it was arduous work and conditions were wretched, with continual rain and insufficient supplies.[71] Nonetheless, it was to Stockenström that the first indications of the submission of the ama-Ndlambe came. Having established a camp on the high ground to the east of the Fish River, overlooking Trompetter's Drift, he was returning from a patrol on the afternoon of 15 August when two emaciated Xhosa women were seen to approach. They were, they revealed, messengers from Nxele: he wished to sue for peace, but would only come in provided his life and liberty were guaranteed. However, while Stockenström was prepared to accede to the first request, the second was out of the question. Nxele must submit and he would be detained.

He was fortunate to be offered that. Nxele and certain other sub-chiefs had a bounty on their heads and Willshire had threatened to continue the campaign down to the 'utter extermination' of the ama-Ndlambe unless they were delivered up. Not that Stockenström expected Nxele to appear. He thought the incident part of a spying expedition. However, the following day Nxele walked into the camp and requested the restoration of peace, in the apparent belief that Stockenström was in command of the colonial forces and held full plenipotentiary powers. Instead, word was sent to Willshire,

---

71   Letter to Colonel C. Bird, 21 Sept. 1819: Hutton (ed.), *Stockenström*, I, p.153. 'There is no need to follow in detail the course of the campaign', wrote Stockenström's biographer, J.L. Dracopoli, *Sir Andries Stockenström 1792–1864: The Origins of the Racial Conflict in South Africa* (Cape Town: A.A. Balkema, 1969), p.46. Indeed, but an indication of its nature would have been pertinent.

CONTROLLING THE FRONTIER

Trompetter's Drift with Fish River in flood. (Cory, *Rise of South Africa* II, 1913)

who came down in person, after which Nxele was conveyed under guard to Colonel Cuyler in Uitenhage.[72]

That part of Fraser's force pursuing the ama-Ndlambe towards the Keiskamma had, in the meantime, been continuing its campaign. No unnecessary risks were taken: the field-pieces would be loosed indiscriminately against those Xhosa found sheltering in the bush, so that before the end of August only stragglers remained west of the river. But no sooner was this achieved than Willshire began co-ordinating plans to cross the Keiskamma and continue the campaign in the stretch of country beyond the Keiskamma and the Buffalo, even as far as the Kei.

Willshire believed that the Xhosa would artfully leave 'all their old lean cows' to be found by a pursuing force, whilst 'driving the fat ones, oxen and horses over the Keiskamma to the Buffels River, not supposing that we would go any further to punish them'. They would, he added, 'know better soon'.[73] There were again restless calls to give chase immediately, including from Stockenström, but the Keiskamma was in flood and Willshire would not let the mounted commandos move on unsupported not only by regular troops, but also the artillery and engineers who had proved invaluable.[74]

---

72   Maclennan, *Proper Degree of Terror*, pp.207–209.
73   Maclennan, *Proper Degree of Terror*, pp.209–210.
74   Hutton (ed.), *Stockenström*, I, pp.153–154.

The plea of Ndlambe's and Nxele's chief councillors/phakathi

Not long after Nxele's surrender, with Stockenström now in company with Willshire, a small party of Xhosa drew near Willshire's camp and signalled their wish for 'a parley'. Stockenström's notes of the occasion, placed at Thomas Pringle's disposal in 1825, appeared in the latter's *Narrative of a Residence in South Africa*. 'The Colonel [Willshire], attended by another officer and myself, having moved towards them unarmed', Stockenström recalled, 'two Caffers approached.' These men proved to be Islambi's (that is, Ndlambe's) and Makanna's (Nxele's) *phakathi* or chief councillors – *phakathi* being the Xhosa equivalent of the Zulu term *induna*/pl. *izinduna*, meaning a high official or adviser/councillor.

Stockenström was startled by their self-possession and coherence. After enquiring after Nxele and 'the prospects of an accommodation', Nxele's 'friend' (as Stockenström described him) 'in so manly a manner, with so graceful an attitude, and with so much feeling and animation, that the bald translation which I am able to furnish from my hasty and imperfect notes, can afford but a very faint and inadequate idea of his eloquence', delivered a sort of homily on how they had arrived at this situation.[75]

You 'British chiefs … are striving to extirpate a people … forced to take up arms', it began in Stockenström's paraphrased translation. 'When our fathers, and the fathers of the Boors (*Amabulu*) first settled in the Zureveld, they dwelt together in peace. Their flocks grazed on the same hills; their herdsmen smoked together out of the same pipes; they were brothers – until the herds of the Amakosa [Xhosa] increased so as to make the hearts of the Boors sore. What those covetous men could not get from our fathers for old buttons, they took by force.' 'Our fathers were MEN', it continued, 'they loved their cattle; their wives and children lived upon milk; they fought for their property.'

Particular objection was made to the continued policy of favouring Ngqika – who was, of course, there at the encampment. 'When there was war, we plundered you', the spokesman acknowledged. 'When there was peace, some of our bad people stole; but our chiefs forbade it. Your treacherous friend, Gaika [Ngqika], always had peace with you; yet, when his people stole, he shared in the plunder. Have your patroles [*sic*] ever found cattle taken in time of peace, runaway slaves, or deserters, in the kraals of *our* [*sic*] chiefs?' he asked rhetorically (although deserters there certainly were). 'Have they ever gone into Gaika's country without finding such cattle, such slaves, such deserters, in Gaika's kraals? But he was your friend; and you wished to possess the Zureveld.' So you 'came at last like locusts' (a reference to Graham's campaign), telling the ama-Ndlambe to cross the Fish River. 'We yielded, and came here', the spokesman observed; but still it went on. Indeed

---

75 Pringle, *Narrative*, p.285. Stockenström's 'notes', and the manner in which he and Pringle frame them, constitute not only an influential, but (in historiographical terms) perhaps the predominant primary document on Xhosa suffering over the course of these years: witness Mostert's 'epic', *Frontiers*, p.485, wherein the address (as Stockenström recorded it) is held up as 'one of most moving declarations in South African history'.

it got worse. (This must have struck a chord with Willshire, who had come to view Ngqika and his followers with increasing mistrust, itself indicative of the inexpediency of the current policy.)

'We lived in peace', the spokesman affirmed: 'Some bad people stole [but] the chiefs were quiet.' By contrast, 'Gaika stole – his chiefs stole – his people stole.' And with what result: 'You sent him copper; you sent him beads; you sent him horses – on which he rode to steal more. To *us* [sic] you sent only commandoes!'[76]

What could they do? 'We quarrelled with Gaika about grass – no business of yours. You sent a commando [Brereton's] – you took our last cow – you left only a few calves, which died for want, along with our children.' Were they supposed just to lie down and die? 'You gave half the spoil to Gaika; half you kept yourselves. Without milk, our corn destroyed, we saw our wives and children perish – we saw that we must ourselves perish; we followed, therefore, the tracks of our cattle into the colony. We plundered, and we fought for our lives.' And they grew in confidence. 'We found you weak … We saw that we were strong; we attacked your head-quarters [Stockenström's translation: a reference to Grahamstown] – and if we had succeeded, our right was good, for you began the war. We failed – and you are here … your troops cover the plains, and swarm in the thickets, where they cannot distinguish the man from the woman, and shoot all.'

'We wish for peace', he concluded, but the colony's continued political interference in Xhosian matters prevented it. 'You want us to submit to Gaika. That man's face is fair to you, but his heart is false.' All they could do was appeal to the colonial government. 'Leave him [Ngqika] to himself. Make peace with us. Let him fight for himself – and *we* [sic] shall not call on you for help. Set Makanna [Nxele] at liberty; and Islambi, Dushani, Kongo, and the rest will come to make peace with you at any time you fix.' To continue would avail the British little: '[Y]ou may indeed kill the last man of us – but Gaika shall not rule over the followers of those who think him a woman.'[77]

'This manly remonstrance', as Pringle called it, reputedly reduced 'some of those who heard it even to tears';[78] but as the two *phakathi* had moved forwards to meet only Willshire, Stockenström and 'another officer', who were alone and unarmed (and presumably out of earshot), this would seem unlikely and can perhaps be understood more accurately as a reflection of how Stockenström and Pringle felt when discussing the affair retrospectively. It made no difference to events at the time. Plans went ahead to cross the Keiskamma in continuance of the campaign.

Across the Keiskamma

The crossing was effected on 9 September 1819. Next day Willshire's force moved forward in the three-column format, Stockenström's commando

---

76   Stockenström's 'notes': Pringle, *Narrative*, pp.285-286.
77   Stockenström's 'notes': Pringle, *Narrative*, pp.286–287.
78   Pringle, *Narrative*, p.287.

THE FIFTH CAPE FRONTIER WAR

A subsequent depiction of close quarters bush fighting on the eastern frontier, by artist and explorer Thomas Baines, 1820-1875. (Museum Africa, previously Africana Museum)

this time forming the left-hand/northern column, sent to the forested area incorporating the sources of the Keiskamma and the Buffalo.

In this difficult terrain, on 11 September (as Stockenström reported), 'I divided my force into several small parties, and entered the forest at all points about daybreak'. There were a number of skirmishes, notably when the Xhosa 'attacked a small party under the Commandant [field cornet/temporary field commandant] Abram Smit of my district [Graaff-Reinet] with fire-arms as well as assegais'; but the burghers fought back well, leaving seven of their assailants 'dead on the spot, independent of the many severely wounded who crept to die in the corner'. 'I was near with twenty men', Stockenström noted, 'and proceeded to the spot', bringing the burgher strength up to fifty, at which point the Xhosa rallied 'and charged once more'. However, they were again halted, after which they 'did not show themselves again that day'.[79] Next day, 12 September, twelve more Xhosa were killed, 'besides those who were severely wounded and must soon have perished'.

Meanwhile Willshire again accompanied the central column, which crossed the Buffalo on 14 September and started for the Kei. Fraser led the right-hand/southern column, which moved up the coast towards the mouth of the Kei. Kobe, who was a son of the late Chungwa of the Gqunukhwebe (and had married a daughter of Ndlambe's), gave himself up to Fraser's column. Of Ndlambe there was no immediate news, but he was running out of options and Stockenström thought that he was on to him. However, Willshire's orders were to maintain an even front. By that time Willshire was in communication with the Xhosa chief Hintsa (the paramount chief of the entire Xhosa nation) who, perturbed at the approach of colonial forces, had

---

79   Hutton (ed.), *Stockenström*, I, p.154.

declared that he would refuse the fleeing ama-Ndlambe refuge and surrender any of their cattle sheltering in his territory.[80]

The question was, therefore: What would Ndlambe do when confronted with this likely impasse? Both Willshire and Stockenström anticipated correctly: denied the opportunity to seek refuge in the trans-Kei, and with the way towards the coast having become the route to entrapment, he had either to surrender or move north. He moved north, and on 16 September Stockenström's commando encountered at least some of the remaining ama-Ndlambe force at the junction of the Kabousie and Kei rivers (the Kabousie running west to east into the Kei).

'My party', Stockenström reported, 'shot a great number, and took 7,000 head of cattle.' Believing that Ndlambe must be within reach – he was with the notorious plunderer, Mnyaluza, for whose apprehension Willshire had offered a reward – Stockenström detached a 300 strong burgher force under his trusted field cornets, Stephanus van Wyk and Tjaart van der Walt. However, they were unable to track the fugitives down and the chance was lost: Ndlambe found refuge in Thembu territory.[81]

Stockenström turned south to rejoin Willshire. The strain was beginning to tell on him, both physically and mentally. In correspondence with the Colonial Secretary in Cape Town, Colonel Christopher Bird, he had developed the slightly undignified habit of (albeit temperately) blaming Willshire for any failings on the part of his own commando, and he was distressed to witness the escalation of fear and unrest along the Kei. Elements of the fleeing ama-Ndlambe had intermingled with, and were being sheltered among, communities that had purportedly participated in the attack on Grahamstown and which undoubtedly harboured white deserters. Ngqika, naturally, did all he could to reinforce these assumptions, wishing to carry the campaign into Hintsa's territory, and it looked for a time like that would be the outcome. Villages were attacked, and when the Xhosa involved fled across the Kei, there was a predisposition to pursue them. However, Stockenström perceived the danger and sought to prevent it.

Stockenström's letter to Colonel Bird

On 21 September 1819, learning from Colonel Willshire's column that a party would be travelling back to the colony next day, Stockenström took the opportunity to detail these events in a letter to Colonel Bird. 'On coming up with the divisions on my right I found that they had come among some of Hintza's Kraals under Boocho, whence the Kaffirs had fled …across the Key', he stated. 'Boocho' was Hintsa's elder brother, Bhurhu, whose kraals were situated relatively close to the Kei (some three hours' travelling distance beyond its banks, whereas Hintsa's Great Place was some nine hours distance: traditionally those wishing to visit Hintsa or enter his country had to explain

---

80   Maclennan, *Proper Degree of Terror*, p.213; Hutton (ed.), *Stockenström*, I, p.154.
81   Maclennan, *Proper Degree of Terror*, p.213; Hutton (ed.), *Stockenström*, I, pp.118, 155.

THE FIFTH CAPE FRONTIER WAR

Xhosa village, aquatint published by Evert Maaskamp, from album *Description physique et historique des Cafres, sur la cote meridionale de l'Afrique*, Amsterdam 1811 (but originally issued as an accompaniment to *De Kaffers aan de Zuidkust van Afrika*, Amsterdam 1810), by Lodewijk Alberti.

British forces crossing the Kei, painting by Thomas Baines. (Museum Africa, previously Africana Museum)

Colonel Christopher Chapman Bird (1769-1861): Colonial Secretary, Cape Colony, 1818-1824. (Cory, *Rise of South Africa* II, 1913)

their business to Bhurhu and be vetted before being granted permission).[82] 'Some shots had been fired among them [Bhurhu's kraals]', Stockenström went on, 'and the slaughter was likely to continue on pretence of their having allowed the enemy to take shelter among them, and their harbouring deserters, and having had a share in the attack made on the Colony.' He therefore gave Colonel Willshire what he called 'my candid opinion' that Ngqika was seeking to involve them in a war with Hintsa.

'I had taken some of Boocho's men and women', Stockenström told Bird, and while it was true that 'a good number' of the enemy had mixed with them, it was something they (Bhurhu's people) were unable to prevent. Similarly, while they admitted that 'white men' had lived among them, in reality they 'dreaded' them and these men had fled on news of the approach of a colonial force.

Therefore Stockenström acquitted them on every count, seeing it as a political imperative to do so. They admitted having 'Colonial cattle and horses in their country', he acknowledged, but only what they had obtained 'from Gaika [Ngqika], Tsambie [Ndlambe], and other ... neighbours in exchange for women, &c.' They 'denied all participation in any outrages against the Colony, which', he added, 'I had no reason to think them guilty of'. As regards Ndlambe's people, he advised Willshire that 'it would even be policy to allow [them] to mix with neutrals in order to weaken his forces' – otherwise they would have 'no alternative but that of adhering to him and sharing in his desperation'. The object was to 'keep Hintza in awe' and that had been achieved. 'Hintza and all under him are in such a state of terror that I am convinced they would not only give up the deserters ... and the Colonial cattle and horses, but even their own cattle to purchase their lives which they consider at our disposal.'[83]

To Colonel Bird, Stockenström characteristically portrays Willshire as being slightly obtuse in respect of all this. However, the evidence does not suggest that to be the case at all. He agreed to Stockenström's communications with Hintsa – with whom there had already been contact. He may have demonstrated a degree of scepticism regarding the claims of complete innocence coming from all sides, not least in the harbouring of deserters, but the implication that Stockenström had in effect to wrest control of the situation from Willshire is not accurate.

---

82 Mostert, *Frontiers*, p.364.
83 Hutton (ed.), *Stockenström*, I, pp.155–157.

In view of what had happened to his father, it was both brave and commendable of Stockenström to seek out Bhurhu, but it cannot be said that he underplayed the drama in his letter to Bird. 'With a vast deal of trouble, at length by going unarmed and alone to a distance from my party I persuaded Boocho to come across the river to me, terrified and trembling', he reported. He then laid down the law to Bhurhu – and, indirectly, Hintsa – just as Willshire had instructed; for, although you would hardly gather it from this letter, Stockenström was in fact acting under Willshire's orders. 'I told him of the object and success of the Commando', Stockenström stated, and 'added that we had come prepared to make them share the same fate with Tsambie [Ndlambe] if they were in the least hostilely inclined; but that … the Governor would not deprive Hintza of any of his rights and possessions if he complied with what was reasonable'.[84]

Bhurhu, not unnaturally, immediately conceded every point, asserting in addition that he 'always acted for [Hintsa] if necessary'. Thus Hintsa, he said, 'had fled to the Bashee, but should be immediately sent for; that the deserters had fled to the Tambookies [Thembu], but should be delivered up if they ever came among them again, and that both he and Hintza would be glad to come to an understanding with Gaika'. Ngqika was in the vicinity and, somewhat prematurely, Stockenström brought these Xhosa chiefs together. The initial meeting, he acknowledged, 'was by no means friendly': Ngqika 'refused to salute or lodge in the same tent' as Bhurhu.

Next morning ('yesterday' morning, as Stockenström put it: that is, 20 September 1819) was little better. What Stockenström called 'old sores' were reopened and 'the argument was hot'. Bhurhu told Ngqika 'to his face' that all the colonial cattle beyond the Kei had been got 'in exchange' from himself and Ndlambe, 'but principally from himself', and he 'defied' Ngqika to accuse Hintsa of having participated in the attack on Grahamstown. However, Ngqika refused to respond, demanding Willshire's presence in any discussions.[85]

For his part, Stockenström was 'convinced' that 'the inhabitants of these parts' had been 'misrepresented to us' and, throwing aside any semblance of discretion, concluded by attributing the whole situation to Willshire's military incompetence. 'I think with due submission to Colonel Willshire's military talents and experience that we … ought to have sent our Cavalry to overtake the enemy before he could get thus far instead of detaining that body on account of the Infantry and baggage', he wrote in reproach of Willshire's strategy – which was for a balanced force to advance on an even front from the sources of the Keiskamma, Buffalo and Kabousie in the north to the coast and the mouth of the Kei in the south. However, given the context, simply to dismiss the supporting arms as 'baggage' (rather like Christiaan de Wet telling recalcitrant commandos in the Boer War to leave their wagons behind) is neither fair nor accurate.

Stockenström's impatience with Willshire had underlined the whole communication with Bird. The implication was that Stockenström would

---

84   Hutton (ed.), *Stockenström*, I, p.157.
85   Hutton (ed.), *Stockenström*, I, pp.157–158.

have brought the campaign to a successful conclusion more swiftly and authoritatively if only Willshire had not interfered. In both tone and timing it was a striking document, and he appears to have feared that he may have been too explicit. 'I find I have unawares deviated from my original determination of making no comment, but confining myself to a simple statement of facts … leaving you to draw your own conclusions', he at one point asserts, not entirely convincingly.

Yet not only did he 'comment', as he put it, he was also at pains to get his comments to Bird at the first opportunity, while matters were still to be concluded and without a period of reflection or, indeed, discussion of these latest developments with Willshire. And as if to place himself at one remove from his actions, while still being complicit in undermining confidence in Willshire, he closed by declaring: 'The conduct of this expedition will be the subject of much correspondence; exaggeration will be employed as well for, as against our leader, but I fear principally against him; therefore my reflections are superfluous.'[86]

Finally he added a few generalised observations on 'the state of things in Kaffirland' in order to 'avoid the imputation of jealousy proceeding from a want of attention to my advice or opinion' – an admission unlikely to detract from that impression. But in any event, Stockenström's relations with the governor, Lord Charles Somerset, were shortly to deteriorate sharply. This letter cannot have enhanced his immediate reputation in Cape Town.

Conclusion of the campaign

Bhurhu may have assured Stockenström that he 'always acted for [Hintsa] if necessary' and that Hintsa would be 'immediately sent for', but whatever Stockenström's assurances, Willshire was not going to conclude the campaign without having a meeting with Hintsa and unambiguously prescribing future acceptable conduct among the Xhosa. Fearfully, Hintsa did come to meet Willshire, after which in keeping with Somerset's policy he was cautioned against continued hostility to Ngqika or any form of collusion with Ndlambe.

Ndlambe was still at large, but his influence and authority were never to recover, and after two months in the field and with the fighting effectively over the Boers on commando began drifting away on their own initiative, leaving Willshire to follow in their wake. His force took away some 30,000 head of cattle, to compensate for losses and help defray the costs of the campaign; but the main achievement, according to Willshire, was to prove to Ndlambe, Ngqika and Hintsa alike that 'no bush can save them from punishment' and that henceforth they should 'value the friendship of the colony'.[87]

Stockenström's apparent contention that Willshire's handling of the expedition would be the subject of disapproval and sanction was not borne out by events. In the aftermath of the campaign, the eastern border of the colony was extended to the Keiskamma River, and on Somerset's instructions the

---

86   Hutton (ed.), *Stockenström*, I, pp.158–159.
87   Maclennan, *Proper Degree of Terror*, pp.216–217.

THE FIFTH CAPE FRONTIER WAR

Hintsa (c.1790-1835), chief of the amaGcaleka and paramount chief of the Xhosa. (Frontispiece from *Narrative of a Voyage of Observation among the Colonies of Western Africa … and of a Campaign in Kaffir-Land on the Staff of the Commander-in-Chief in 1835*, Vol. I, by James Edward Alexander [London: Henry Colburn, 1837], with maps and plates by Major Charles Collier Michell, 1793-1851: Surveyor General and Civil Engineer, Cape of Good Hope, 1828; Assistant Quartermaster General, Sixth Frontier War, 1834-35)

construction of a fort – Fort Willshire – was begun at the confluence of the Keiskamma and Ngqakayi rivers, to guard the approaches to the ceded territory. Then when Willshire did eventually leave the Cape (for India) in 1822, he received promotion without purchase in reward for his services. He subsequently gained distinction commanding a column of the 'Army of the Indus' during the First Afghan War.[88]

As for Nxele, after his being transferred to Cape Town, Somerset determined that he should be incarcerated on Robben Island, but otherwise treated with both kindness and respect. He was given a furnished apartment and provided with whatever food he required; but on the night of 9 August 1820, in company with some 30 fellow prisoners, he attempted to escape in a whaling boat. He never made it. The vessel capsized off Blouebergstrand and he drowned. Few among the Xhosa believed it – not even Ngqika. Before he

Fort Willshire, from a lithograph (erroneously labelled 'Caffer Fair Fort Wiltshire') in Andrew Steedman, *Wanderings and Adventures in the Interior of Southern Africa* (London: Longman & Co., 1835)

---

88   DSAB II, p.849; Low, *Soldiers of the Victorian Age*, pp.74–104.

gave himself up to Willshire's forces, Nxele had vowed that one day he would return, and that promise became ingrained in Xhosa culture, its overtones evident in the emergence of the tragic cattle-killing movement over three decades later.[89]

Neither John Graham nor George Fraser outlived him by long. In October 1820 Graham was appointed first landdrost of the new district of Albany, but illness forced his resignation within weeks, and he died, aged 42, on 17 March 1821. Fraser died at his farm, Lombard's Post, south of Grahamstown, on 19 October 1823.

Frontier settlers

In the aftermath of the Fifth Cape Frontier War of 1818–1819, Lord Charles Somerset had abandoned the Fish River boundary and instead demanded from the Xhosa chief Ngqika, 'as the price of [colonial] military assistance', what J.B. Peires described as 'the rich lands between the Fish and the Keiskamma River'. It was a decision that had profound consequences. By effectively confiscating the land 'where Ngqika himself had always resided' the colonial government not only alienated Ngqika in the short term, but also his sons – and in particular Maqoma. No longer would frontier unrest be confined to what Peires, with perhaps too little regard to the intensity of the recent struggle, characterised as 'the relatively minor chiefs of the western outposts of Xhosaland', with Ngqika more or less tolerating colonial attacks on rebellious subordinates. The 'scope of the military struggle on the colonial frontier' would in future to be 'immensely broadened'.[90]

And then there was the question of the administration of the sequestrated land – both as regards the initial purpose of the sequestration, and the subsequent allocation of the land. The course of events was, in fact, subject early on to no little obfuscation. 'One of the hardy minor myths of South African history', Peires has noted, 'is that Somerset intended to create a "neutral belt" of open territory between colonist and Xhosa.' This was not so. The reality was that his official dispatch had specifically referred to the land as 'ceded', and had moreover included a strong recommendation to the Colonial Secretary, Lord Bathurst, that it be utilised for 'systematic colonisation'. The subsequent ambiguity and obfuscation had resulted largely from Somerset's bitter feud with General Sir Rufane Donkin, the acting governor from January 1820 to November 1821 during Somerset's leave of absence. Donkin established a controversial settlement in the ceded territory, and Somerset

---

89   Maclennan, *Proper Degree of Terror*, pp.220–221; DSAB I, p.597; Peires, *The Dead Will Arise*, pp.1–2. For a more recent study stressing 'the popular heroic view of Makhanda [Nxele] as one of South Africa's early freedom fighters' see J.C. Wells, *The Return of Makhanda: Exploring the Legend* (Scottsville: University of KwaZulu-Natal Press, 2012), although Mostert had essentially already done that.

90   J.B. Peires, 'The British and the Cape, 1814–1834', in R. Elphick and H. Giliomee (eds), *The Shaping of South African Society, 1652–1840* (Cape Town: Maskew Miller Longman, 1989), pp.482–483.

on learning of it claimed that it ran counter to his policy of establishing a neutral belt.[91]

As far back as 1809 Major Richard Collins, whom Caledon had appointed commissioner of the frontier districts, had recommended that an increased white population be settled along the Fish River in order to stabilise the border region, and the proposal would periodically re-emerge in one guise or another throughout the next decade. Colonel Graham was drawn to the idea in the aftermath of the Fourth Cape Frontier War, and there was some limited discussion of the subject with Sir John Cradock. Thus Henry Alexander, the Colonial Secretary to the Cape Government, wrote to Graham on 23 May 1812 that 'it is His Excellency's intention you should encourage settlers in the Zuure Berg or wherever you please', always bearing in mind that the object was to encourage not merely 'grazing and an indolent … life' (a reference to the Boers), but rather 'progressive civilisation, agricultural improvement and common defence'.[92]

Therefore, when on leave in Britain, Colonel Graham submitted (21 May 1813) a proposal that 500 highland crofters be settled in the Zuurveld. And it was a measure of how well connected Graham was – notably through his kinsman, General Sir Thomas Graham – that in November 1813 he persuaded the newly appointed governor of the Cape, Lord Charles Somerset, to pursue the matter directly with Lord Bathurst at the War and Colonial Office.

In a letter of 29 November, written from his London residence (Bruton Street), from where he was preparing to leave for the Cape, Somerset asserted: 'Your Lordship is so fully aware of the importance and utility of increasing the population' that 'I should venture without apology' to submit for consideration any viable plan to that end. He therefore took the liberty of forwarding a copy of Graham's submission to Henry Alexander 'showing the expedience of removing some of the families from the Highlands of Scotland to the Cape'. It was, he stated, due 'more than an ordinary show of consideration' – which amounted to as strong an endorsement as protocol allowed.[93]

In the event, the proposal was not adopted. However, when just a few years later, in 1817, Benjamin Moodie of Melsetter in the Orkney Islands brought 200 unmarried Scottish artisans to the Cape as part of a private venture, such was the demand for skilled labour that the scheme ultimately proved successful. Lord Charles Somerset, in keeping with Graham's previous proposal, wanted to settle these men in the Zuurveld to help stabilise the frontier, but Moodie would not countenance so exposed an environment, so official support was withdrawn. But it encouraged Somerset to renew his calls to London for an official immigration scheme – which, as a result of pressures generated within the United Kingdom, Lord Bathurst was now predisposed to accept.[94]

---

91 Peires, 'The British and the Cape', p.438.
92 H. Alexander to Graham, 23 May 1812: C.T. Atkinson (ed.), *Manuscripts of Robert Graham Esq. of Fintry*, p.120.
93 Millar, *Plantagenet in South Africa*, p.51.
94 Millar, *Plantagenet in South Africa*, pp.103–104.

This was the genesis of the 1820 Settlers scheme, which had such a profound and far-reaching effect on the eastern Cape and, over time, southern Africa more widely. Ironically, Somerset was on leave in England when the Settlers began to arrive in April 1820 and the arrangements for their reception and distribution (west of the Fish River) were left to the acting governor, Sir Rufane Donkin. These arrangements were wholly inadequate, resulting in considerable hardship. It would take some years for all frontier communities to adapt to the situation, including with the emergence of licensed trading with the Xhosa, for ivory and skins, from Fort Willshire.

Somerset/Donkin dispute

Somerset thought matters had been so disposed that Donkin would take care only to follow settled administrative instructions and procedures. But in fact Donkin blithely declined to follow set procedures in a number of areas. This may have stemmed in some measure from his pronounced Whig sympathies, but he was a difficult, depressive and at times unbalanced man, who seemed to embrace political and personal confrontation – never difficult to engender with the Somersets under any circumstances. Indeed, his subsequent behaviour would suggest that he imagined himself as a contemporary Philip Francis to Somerset's Warren Hastings (with Henry Brougham in the role of Edmund Burke), and he ultimately took his own life.[95]

Among Donkin's initiatives was an attempt to make Bathurst the centre of the newly independent district of Albany in place of Grahamstown and abandoning the region's envisaged defence scheme (stopping work on Fort Willshire). But not least provoking – to Somerset – was Donkin's decision to initiate his own settlement scheme, beginning by settling some of the men of the disbanded Royal African Corps in the ceded territory between the Great Fish and Keiskamma rivers. Somerset was so outraged by Donkin's presumption that, as seen, on learning of it he claimed that the decision ran counter to his policy of establishing a neutral belt and thereby violated his agreement with Ngqika.

The disbanded Royal African Corps settlement

By contrast with the 60th Regiment, which had been removed from the Cape in January 1819, it had been decided that the Royal African Corps should be disbanded. It fell to Donkin to arrange this, but it was a more problematic process than might first appear. Some rank and file joined the 38th Foot. Others were considered such incorrigible rogues that they could not safely be discharged into the colony. These were drafted into the 72nd Foot, after which they might be employed in manual labour. As Donkin explained: 'I have attached these worthless and unmanageable people to the detachment of the

---

95 Millar, *Plantagenet in South Africa*, pp.122–123, 131, 267–268; DSAB III, pp.234–235.

THE FIFTH CAPE FRONTIER WAR

Lord Charles Somerset as a captain/lieutenant colonel of the Coldstream Guards (a captaincy in the Guards was equivalent to a lieutenant-colonelcy in another regiment), by the leading portrait painter of the Regency period, Richard Cosway, RA (1742-1821)

Lieutenant General Sir Rufane Shaw Donkin (1772-1841), Acting Governor, Cape Colony, January 1820 to November 1821. (Stipple engraving of 1831 executed by 'W. Holl' – William Holl, father or son – from a painting by Henry Mayer, c.1782-1847)

72nd Regiment at Grahamstown, but I shall take the earliest opportunity I can of removing them to Cape Town, as neither the settlers nor the ordinary inhabitants here would be safe in the vicinity of such congregated banditti as these men will form when collected.' These men, Cory tells us, were formed into two companies in which they not only 'kept out of mischief', but also performed a 'most useful service to the Colony by constructing the road over the Fransche Hoek Pass' before eventually being transferred to Sierra Leone in 1823.[96]

With the remainder, who might be entrusted with their liberty, Donkin decided to establish a military village in the territory between the Great Fish and Keiskamma rivers. A site was selected on the right bank of the Begha River, 'a few miles' south-east of present-day Peddie (where Ndlambe's Great Place had previously been located), 'probably very near where the village of Woolridge now stands'; but a significant distribution of land would also be involved.[97] The settlement was to be named Fredericksburg, in honour of HRH Prince Frederick, Duke of York and Albany ('the Grand Old Duke of

---

96 Cory, *Rise of South Africa*, II (London: Longmans, Green & Co., 1913), p.108.
97 Cory, *Rise of South Africa*, II, pp.109–110. The Begha River (previously spelt 'Beka') is also known as the Bequa, Bira or Birha.

CONTROLLING THE FRONTIER

'Canteen scene during the frontier wars', oil painting by F.T. I'Ons, of which at least two full copies were made by the Cape Town artist W.H.F.L. Langschmidt (1805-1866). (Fehr Collection, Castle of Good Hope)

York'). Ten officers and 78 men were to initiate the scheme, and they were to be joined by Benjamin Moodie, the organiser of the 1817 settler scheme, together with his brothers, Donald and J. Dunbar Moodie. Whatever its origins, if successful, the reality would be an extension of the system of colonisation being undertaken both behind and beyond the Fish River.

With a 33 strong detachment from the Cape Corps stationed on site, the first settlers arrived in June 1820. By the end of July, 17 well-constructed houses had reportedly been completed as part of the settlement. But it was not to prosper. Its situation was isolated and exposed and the dispossessed Xhosa could hardly fail to feel aggrieved at this usurpation of their land. In short, neutral belt or not, the establishment of such a settlement was a provocation. Moreover, the terms under which the soldiers were to settle were never satisfactorily resolved, and when Somerset withdrew any military protection on his return to the colony in December 1821, the outpost effectively disintegrated. Many men simply wandered back to the colony without authorisation, to gain what employment they could. Others, hardly surprisingly, began an illicit trade with the Xhosa. By April 1822, according to an official report, the Fredericksburg settlement consisted of just three private soldiers. Within a short time it was abandoned altogether. The Moodie brothers were granted land in the Zuurveld.[98]

---

98 Cory, *Rise of South Africa*, II, pp.110–112; DSAB II, p.488.

3

Colonial Forces Beyond the Frontier: The Fetcani Alarm

Lord Charles Somerset as Governor of the Cape of Good Hope maintained a strong interest in the affairs of the Cape Corps, not least through the influence of his eldest son, Henry Somerset. When on leave in England in 1820, Lord Charles argued that the Corps was the unit best suited to the unique demands of border warfare and that it should consequently be both strengthened and properly equipped. Indeed, he took it upon himself to requisition the necessary uniforms for the Corps, even specifying that a service waistcoat should be added to meet the cold conditions at times prevailing on the frontier. But, as in other areas, his deputy at the Cape, Acting Governor Sir Rufane Donkin, did all in his power to undermine his proposals. Donkin suggested to the War and Colonial Office that it would be better to augment regular British forces at the Cape – a flawed judgement, motivated to some degree at least by jealously and an intense antipathy to the Somersets, and from which even his own civil servants distanced themselves.[1]

Whatever Donkin's motives, the dispute did little to help Lord Charles Somerset's efforts to increase the Corps' strength, and in particular its mounted strength. Somerset addressed a lengthy dispatch to the Secretary of State for War and the Colonies, Lord Bathurst, on 10 December 1822, pleading to be given the authority to increase the cavalry element of the Corps and then equip this element with the double-barrelled carbines that he had ordered while on leave in England. The matter had, indeed, become imperative to him, for just two days later, on 12 December, he reiterated emphatically to the Commandant of the Frontier, Lieutenant Colonel Maurice Scott, that: 'Whenever it may be necessary to follow the Kaffirs into Kaffraria or to make any attacks on them, it must only be done by the Cavalry Mounted Infantry [*sic*] or Mounted Burghers. The Infantry', he went on, 'are useless on these occasions and must be entirely employed as defence or scouring the Bush.'[2]

---

1   D.E. Rivett-Carnac, *Hawk's Eye: Lieutenant-General Sir Henry Somerset K.C.B., K.H.* (Cape Town: Howard Timmins, 1966), p.36.
2   Rivett-Carnac, *Hawk's Eye*, p.41.

The problem was, what he called the 'Mounted Burghers', could only be called out in an emergency, whereas the situation demanded the permanent policing of the frontier. Bathurst conceded the point and in March 1823 sanctioned the addition of two troops of cavalry to the Cape Corps, further stipulating that the commanding officer of the Corps should in future be stationed permanently on the frontier, there to give matters his undivided attention. The new cavalry troops were duly organised by the then Major Henry Somerset, who sought out specimens of 'Dragoon Horse' for their use.

Being on active service by the close of 1823 these cavalry troops quickly proved their worth in the field, but numbers were still insufficient and the colony experienced considerable difficulties in bearing the costs of even that number – a burden that the War and Colonial Office was reluctant to share. The members of the commission of inquiry, appointed in 1823 to investigate the administration of the Cape, admitted Lord Charles Somerset's view that, in the latter's words, 'the innate habits of the Hottentot and his tact in detecting the wily cunning of the Kaffir render him much more available than a European for [the] peculiar and very harassing service' of frontier policing,[3] but found that unless the British government would agree to underwrite its continued maintenance, the Corps could not long continue in its present form.

Thus on 14 June 1826 the commissioners recommended that the Cape Corps' most expensive element, the cavalry, be reduced. This would, it was calculated, lower the annual cost of the Corps from £28,088 to £21,143. It was a recommendation that not only ran counter to reforms adopted only after much lobbying some three years earlier, if implemented it would also self-evidently undermine the unit's effectiveness. Lord Bathurst therefore rejected the proposal, preferring instead to disband the Corps altogether.

A regular regiment would seemingly have to be provided from the British army. But as none was immediately available, an additional military and financial burden was placed on the Boers, who received no pay and had to provide their own guns and horses while they fulfilled ever more persistent demands for their services. Fortunately Richard Bourke, who had become acting governor of the colony on Lord Charles Somerset's return to Great Britain in March 1826, was not unaware of the dangers and on his own initiative he had overseen the drawing-up of plans for 'a Corps of Mounted Riflemen', which would, he perceived, have the advantage of being smaller, cheaper to maintain and better suited to the needs of the colony then either the former Cape Corps or the permanent stationing of a regular regiment. Lord Bathurst presently adopted this draft proposal and on 25 November 1827 the infantry companies were abolished and the old Cape Regiment/Corps was reorganised as a sort of synthesised

---

3   A direct quote from Lord Charles Somerset's plea to retain the Corps: Rivett-Carnac, *Hawk's Eye*, p.58.

A sergeant of The Cape Mounted Rifles, depicted by Thomas Baines. (Museum Africa, previously Africana Museum)

Lieutenant Colonel (later General Sir) Henry Somerset, 1794-1862, eldest son of Lord Charles Somerset and first commanding officer, Cape Mounted Rifles. (19th century lithograph, artist unknown: National Library of South Africa, Cape Town)

cavalry unit, The Cape Mounted Rifles, to be paid for by the Imperial Government.[4]

The new regiment drilled as cavalry and carried swords, but were paid as infantry and employed the double-barrelled S.B. percussion carbine, which continued in service until rifled barrels were introduced in 1854. Both a colour and a guidon were presented and, as befitted the unit's title, dark green jackets and caps were worn, similar in all essentials to those of the celebrated Rifle Brigade in the British army, but with the addition of buff leather trousers. The pouch belt badge also consisted of the rifleman's familiar Maltese cross. Colonel Henry Somerset became the regiment's first commanding officer, although the appointment was not made until June 1828. Major (later Lieutenant Colonel) William Cox, a fellow rifleman of Harry Smith during the Peninsular War, who had served as a captain in a Cape Corps cavalry troop from 1824 to 1826, then served as CO from 1829 to 1834, after which Somerset was to command the regiment again.[5]

---

4   Rivett-Carnac, *Hawk's Eye*, pp.64-65; H. King, *Richard Bourke* (Melbourne: Oxford University Press, 1971), p.77.
5   Rivett-Carnac, *Hawk's Eye*, p.68; Cory, *Rise of South Africa*, II, p.351; Tylden, *Armed Forces of South Africa*, p.57.

The Fetcani alarm

The regiment was soon not only embroiled in the violent complexities of the frontier, but also in the evolving events of the hugely disputed period of the *mfecane*. Remnants of displaced tribes, for the most part Sotho-speaking refugees known collectively as the Mantatee or Mantatees, found their way to the south-west (as well as west and north-west towards Bechuanaland) in the mid 1820s, and by 1825 hundreds of starving refugees had crossed into the districts of Graaff-Reinet and Somerset. Lord Charles Somerset sanctioned their enrolment as apprentices to non-slave holders; however, any further influxes were officially discouraged.

It was one of the first signs of disturbing and little understood events occurring beyond the colony's frontiers. By 1825 the extending chain of warfare and raiding between the northern Nguni societies, of which the Zulu were the most prominent, had begun to impinge on the eastern areas of the Transkei region, as additional rumours of unknown warrior tribes and fugitive hordes reached the borders of the colony.

That year Lieutenant Rogers of the Cape Corps led a first expedition to discover what was causing numbers of Tambookies or Thembu to flee towards the colony.[6] Tambookieland, or Thembuland as it was later known, was the less contentious frontier region to the east of the Tarka district, and centred upon the sources of the Black (*Zwart*) and White (*Wit*) Kei rivers. Little was known of the region, although the year before, in 1824, the missionary John Brownlee had undertaken a pioneering journey through the eastern Xhosa territory, in the course of which he eventually travelled up as far as the kraal of the paramount chief of the Thembu, Ngubengcuka – better known among the Europeans as Vusani.

Lieutenant Roger's expedition discovered little, but noted the climate of fear. So, in September 1826 Colonel Henry Somerset led a small force on a reconnaissance mission to the Tambookie territory around the Stormberg Spruit and Klaas Smits River, near present day Queenstown. But again, all he could discover were abandoned farms and, surprisingly, even what he called Bushmen seeking protection[7]; in other words, circumstantial evidence of the fear and trepidation apparently emanating from the north. All else was rumour, although Steenkamp, field cornet of the Tarka district, had reported that on a patrol shortly before he had himself seen 'thousands of Tambookies

---

6   The label 'Tamboekie' or 'Tambookies' probably derived from the word *Tamboe*, with the '-kie' suffix being a derivative of the Khoikhoi '-*qua*', meaning domain. (It has also been suggested that it derived from the Dutch diminutive suffix '-kje', but that is unlikely, being an inappropriate usage.) Similarly, the term 'Mambookies', in reference to the Mpondo, was derived from the Xhosa *amaMob*, meaning 'nation of the east', with the addition of the '-kie' suffix: Fast (ed.), *Shrewsbury*, p.190fn.115.

7   They may or may not have been San as it was later understood. The Boers used the term *Bosjesmans Kaffers* for isolated Africans who inhabited difficult to reach locations, and Somerset could well have followed that usage: B.J. Liebenberg, *Andries Pretorius, Voortrekker Leader in Natal: Blood River to Congella, 1838-1842*, translated and revised by H. Driver (London: Barksdale Books, 2020), pp.173, 192, 212; J.B. Wright, *Bushman Raiders of the Drakensberg 1840-1870: A Study of their conflict with stock-keeping peoples in Natal 1840-1870* (Pietermaritzburg: University of Natal Press, 1971), p.45fn.51.

lying dead', having seemingly been killed by the mysterious marauders, who had come to be known as the 'Ficani' or 'Fetcani'.[8]

'Fetcani' is a term of considerable imprecision, being little more than an abstract label, originally used (at least among the Europeans) simply to describe any aggressive unsettled or wandering tribe or tribes, or indeed as a noun denoting a military unit of the same. As with the later widespread use of the word *Mfecane*, it stemmed from use of the Xhosa root/suffix '-*feca*', meaning 'to crack', as in to crack and break down maize stalks, and thus was a reference to an aggressor. Therefore, on his return to Grahamstown, Colonel Somerset dispatched a well-supplied mounted force under Major Andrews to probe deep into the Transorange, well beyond the colony's frontiers. This force was accompanied by a number of frontier Boers, and established a river post on the north bank of the Orange, at its junction with the Stormberg Spruit, before following the course of the Caledon River north and eventually bearing east into territory being – unbeknown to them – occupied by the southern Sotho people coalescing under the leadership of Moshoeshoe (alternatively spelt Moshweshwe). Arriving in the area where the Morija mission station would presently be established, they came across a deserted village and presently three assegai-carrying natives who seemingly spoke a Nguni dialect. However, the information Major Andrews derived from them did little to clarify events. At first the members of the expedition thought that they must have come across a village of the mysterious Fetcani, but these Africans told of how they themselves had been harassed by other tribes and were the subjects of a boy king called Maketa. Thus even this expedition had been unable to ascertain the cause of the distant unrest.[9] In reality, the most prominent of the invading tribes would appear (in retrospect) to have been the Bhaca – whose chief, Madikane, had a fearsome reputation, which included burning opponents alive in their huts, but who was killed fighting against the Tambookies/Thembu in December 1824.[10]

None of this seemed to matter greatly over the following months, as little more was heard of such disturbances; but in July 1827 Field Cornet Steenkamp reported to the landdrost of Somerset East, W.M. Mackay, that the Fetcani were again raiding the Tambookies. Some 300 head of cattle had been taken from the sub-chief 'Galela' (Mtyelela) of the Thembu amaGcina clan, and refugees were once more reported to be crossing into the colony, bringing their families and cattle with them.

Sceptical of tales emanating from the Tambookies, but aware of their tendency nonetheless to panic, Mackay would brook no delays. He took it upon himself to investigate these reports, without the aid of the Commandant of the Frontier, Colonel Somerset, whose duties he thereby effectively usurped. Furthermore, he wrote directly to the Government Secretary in

---

8   Cory, *Rise of South Africa*, II, pp.236–237, 344–345; J.B. Peires, 'Matiwane's Road to Mbholompo: A Reprieve for the Mfecane?' in C. Hamilton (ed.), *The Mfecane Aftermath: Reconstructive Debates in Southern African History* (Johannesburg & Pietermaritzburg: Witwatersrand University Press, 1995), pp.221–222, 236-237.
9   Cory, *Rise of South Africa*, II, p.345.
10 Peires, 'Matiwane's Road to Mbholompo', p.222.

Cape Town on the matter, completely bypassing Somerset, an action that was always likely to cause offence, and indeed did.

Leading a small Boer commando, Mackay set off into the Upper Kei region, where he successfully met up with Galela (Mtyelela). After questioning him, Mackay concluded that Steenkamp's report had been accurate: some 300 cattle had evidently been stolen in a raid on the night of 14 July 1827, and a great many Tambookies were on the move towards the colony. As to who was behind the unrest, Galela gave few clues. He told of how he had followed the spoor of the cattle next morning in the direction of the Stormberg range to the Hanglip Mountains, from which were seen large numbers of the marauders gathered on the plain beyond. These were taken to be the Fetcani. But when Mackay then got Galela to take him there, the plain was clear.

However, they did come upon a straggler, and from him a clearer picture at last emerged. He had come from groups dwelling in the Transorange and divided into two tribes: the Masootoo under Maketa, the chief identified by Major Andrews's expedition into the Transorange the year before, and apparently the 'Manguana' or Ngwane under 'Mattuana' (Matiwane), a tribe more usually associated with the Natal region. The marauders' main kraal, according to the captive, was some five days' travelling distance from Galela's, and they had in time fought and raided many tribes with evident success, but were no match for the Zulus under Shaka. To the Zulu they had lost all their own cattle.

It remained a volatile and potentially dangerous situation, as was soon demonstrated; for while Mackay was questioning this straggler, a body of Masootoo-cum-Ngwane warriors came into view driving a herd of captured cattle. Fortunately they abandoned the cattle and fled on seeing the small commando, but Mackay was himself firm in not pursuing the marauders, or allowing Galela (Mtyelela) to, for he had no authority to become involved in a native dispute outside either his own or indeed the colony's jurisdiction – a position that was, of course, to be reversed shortly afterwards, when Maqoma became involved in Tambookie/Thembu affairs, and which controversially led to his expulsion from the Kat River valley. Instead, Mackay prudently withdrew. He reported to the government and, belatedly, Colonel Somerset in a dispatch dated 8 August 1827.[11]

By that time inaction was no longer an option. Some 3,000 Tambookies/Thembu under the restive sub-chief 'Powana' (otherwise known as 'Bawana') had entered the district of Somerset with an estimated 12,000 cattle, and there was further unrest to the south. The insurgents, still referred to as Fetcani, were known to be advancing towards the Chumie [Tyhume] River, which joins the Keiskamma. There was little interference at this stage from the Xhosa. Thus it appeared that the district of Albany was itself threatened. Between them Colonel Somerset and the landdrost, Major William B. Dundas, placed the district in a state of defence, and at one stage Colonel Somerset even proposed calling upon the aid of a Xhosa army under Maqoma's command. But on 31 August 1827, just as all was set for a combined advance against

---

11   Cory, *Rise of South Africa*, II, pp.346–347, 379; Laband, *The Land Wars*, pp.163, 167.

the 'Fetcani', intelligence was received that the insurgents were moving back to the north-east, apparently satisfied with their gains from raids upon both the Tambookies and Xhosa. In retrospect, what had been experienced was probably an armed Ngwane reconnaissance into the region.[12]

It was shortly after this scare that the Cape Corps was disbanded. But the 'Fetcani' troubles were not over, and just a year later were to involve the newly formed Cape Mounted Rifles regiment, operating under Colonel Somerset's direction, in its first serious action.

Clashes on the Umtata: the Dundas commando

The following year saw a series of extraordinary developments. On 4 May 1828, a curious-looking schooner came to rest at the anchorage of Port Elizabeth. It had been constructed in some measure from the wreckage of the *Mary*, which had come to grief on the bar at Port Natal some three years before, and sailed under the name of the *Elizabeth and Susan*. But still more unusual were the passengers conveyed within it, for they included eight Zulus in native dress and a small number of Europeans, one or two in the crude apparel resulting from years spent in near isolation among the Zulu. Unexpectedly, unprepared for – and to the inhabitants of the port, bizarrely – an embassy had arrived from the Zulu chief, Shaka.

Head of the embassy was the senior Zulu *induna*, Sothobe kaMpangalala, with the Port Natal settler James Saunders King acting in the role of guide and intermediary. Lieutenant Francis Farewell and Nathaniel Isaacs were also among the party. At Uitenhage there was a meeting with the landdrost, Van der Riet, who learnt that it was Shaka's apparent wish that Sothobe should visit England both to advise Shaka's 'brother', George IV, of Shaka's friendship and, more pertinently, to establish how his projected destruction of the Mpondo and associated tribes would correlate with His Majesty's concerns as the other paramount ruler in that part of the world. How far the traders at Port Natal had influenced Shaka's actions, in the hope of drawing the British authorities and the Zulu state closer together, thereby gaining recognition of their territorial claims and boosting their own commercial interests, must be a matter of speculation.

The issues raised by the embassy were clearly a matter for the Acting Governor in Cape Town, and Van der Riet duly wrote to the Government Secretary, in the meantime ordering the Resident Magistrate at Port Elizabeth, Captain Francis Evatt (a much respected figure, who had served with the 21st Light Dragoons in the Fourth Frontier War), to accommodate the visiting party. But Van der Riet either did not fully appreciate the urgency of the situation, or failed sufficiently to convey that sense of urgency to the Governor, for General Bourke responded by requesting that the party continue on to Cape Town. Given that Shaka had been prepared to wait just two months before launching his army south, James Saunders King, as

---

12 Cory, *Rise of South Africa*, II, pp.347–350; Peires, 'Matiwane's Road to Mbholompo', pp.229–230.

CONTROLLING THE FRONTIER

General Sir Richard Bourke 1777-1855, Acting Governor of the Cape 1826-1828. (1829 lithograph, artist unknown)

intermediary, found himself in an awkward position. The plan had been for the lesser *induna*, Mbozamboza (sometimes spelt Umbosombozo), to report back as quickly as possible, at which point Henry Fynn, one of the earliest white traders, who had first arrived at Shaka's court in 1824, was to be released – having supposedly stood hostage for the safety of the Zulu representatives. King therefore declined to leave Port Elizabeth, and this static state of affairs lasted some weeks before being overtaken by events. Even before the two months were up, Shaka had dispatched his warriors.

On 12 June 1828 the Rev. W.J. Shrewsbury wrote to the then Civil Commissioner of Albany and Somerset, Major Dundas (who was, in fact, on the point of resigning the position and being replaced by Captain Duncan Campbell), from the Wesleyan mission station at Butterworth. Situated to the east of the Great Kei River, some 200 miles from Grahamstown, this station had been established only the year before to be near the site of Hintsa's Great Place, and had the effect of creating a permanent link between the Cape Colony and the Xhosa paramount. Drafted with commendable moderation, the letter nonetheless contained intelligence of a profoundly alarming nature. Shrewsbury informed Dundas that he had received information the previous evening 'from various quarters, and officially from the Chief, Hintsa', that Shaka's army was advancing, and that he (Shrewsbury) conceived it his duty to advise Dundas of this so that 'the Colonists may neither be alarmed by exaggerated reports that may reach them, nor surprised by any sudden approach of an enemy not to be despised'. Already Shaka had crossed the Umzimvubu (St Johns), about 150 miles from the mission station, and he was known to be approaching with 'a very numerous body of men'. Indeed, Shrewsbury understood the invading force to be divided into eight companies, each consisting of as many as 2,000 to 3,000 warriors. As a result, the whole population in their path was 'described as being in motion'. Shaka's 'avowed object' was, he believed, to reach Hintsa 'as early as possible'.[13]

It should be noted that the year before, in July 1827, Shrewsbury had reported as many as 5,000 to 6,000 Mfengu (hungry/wandering) people around the Butterworth mission station, and that he was even then aware of Shaka as the likely or ultimate instigator of this migration of 'many fragments of tribes, called Fingoes' (Mfengu). How far this understanding, which he had derived from local intelligence, was true or not is not the immediate

---

13   Cory, *Rise of South Africa*, II, pp.354–355; Mostert, *Frontiers*, pp.607–608.

point – although, at least to that extent, Shrewsbury actually had a very good intelligence source in Nicholas Lochenberg, described by William Shaw as 'a Dutch Boor, who had been nearly thirty years expatriated' and who 'with his mulatto family' had a settlement 'in a secluded place near the coast in the territory of Hintsa' (not unlike Fynn with Shaka, Lochenberg had rendered to Hintsa 'assistance with his gun in war and in hunting'). What is germane is that the Zulu were known to be strong and warlike, and that this subsequent direct Zulu involvement in the region was not some similar knock-on effect, but – rightly or wrongly – seen to be altogether different and potentially more consequential for the entire Transkei province.[14]

This intelligence was immediately brought before the advisory council at Cape Town, which had been formed some three years before and which by this time included two nominated burghers, as well as the Acting Governor, the Chief Justice, the Colonial Secretary, the Officer Commanding, the Deputy Quartermaster General, the Auditor General and the Treasurer. Shrewsbury was a respected figure, morally conservative and in that respect judgemental, but not at that time noticeably given to political hyperbole or easily cowed from any quarter – as was well known from his previous experience as a missionary in Barbados. (In October 1823 his chapel at Bridgetown had been burnt-out by what was described as 'a party of respectable gentlemen' on account of what were alleged to be 'unmerited and unprovoked attacks' on the white community. The prominent 1820 Settler, Thomas Philipps, referred to him in March 1829 as 'the celebrated Mr. Shrewsbury who was so ill used at Barbadoes'.) However, perhaps even then there was some latent tendency to overstatement, for by the advent of the Sixth Cape Frontier War (1834–1835) he had become appreciably more disproportionate in his stance on frontier activities. By then he had transferred to the eastern Cape, and having grown increasingly impatient with what he saw as, specifically, Xhosa immorality and aggression, he actively promoted the draconian methods with which the colonial authorities prosecuted the war.[15]

The advisory council, in turn, resolved that it was 'expedient to retain the Caffres within their actual limits', by which they meant primarily those tribes inhabiting what was known as Mpondoland and its surrounding districts, but which, by extension, also referred to the Xhosa. This intention should therefore be conveyed to Shaka, 'with the view of averting his intended invasion'. But should it not be possible to deter him – and such intelligence as was in their possession strongly suggested that it was already too late – then

---

14   Fast (ed.), *Shrewsbury*, pp.37, 187–188 (footnotes 81–83); C. Sadler (ed.), *Never a Young Man: Extracts from the Letters and Journals of the Rev. William Shaw* (Cape Town: HAUM, 1967), p.70.

15   A. Keppel-Jones (ed.), *Philipps, 1820 Settler: His Letters* (Pietermaritzburg: Shuter & Shooter, 1960), p.352; for Shrewsbury's wider background see A. Cobley, 'Sarah Ann Gill's Pastor: Hero or Villain? The Reverend William Shrewsbury in Barbados and South Africa', paper delivered as the Fifth Annual Sarah Ann Gill Memorial Lecture, at the Frank Collymore Hall, Bridgetown, Barbados, 11 May 2011, ResearchGate.net/publication/313302119; and D. Lambert & A. Lester, 'Missionary politics and the captive audience: William Shrewsbury in the Caribbean and the Cape Colony', in Lambert and Lester (eds), *Colonial Lives Across the British Empire: Imperial Careering in the Long Nineteenth Century* (Cambridge: Cambridge University Press, 2006), pp.88–112.

efforts should be made to 'encourage the Caffres to resistance'. This was to be achieved by letting it be known that 'in a case of absolute necessity and on the approach of the Zoolas' they could expect assistance from the colonial government.[16]

The responsibility for carrying these instructions into effect fell upon Colonel Somerset and Major Dundas, men who, notwithstanding their military experience (an artillery officer, Dundas had lost an arm at Badajoz in 1812, while Somerset was mentioned in dispatches at Waterloo), retained a strong distrust of each other and had never worked well together. Somerset immediately placed his troops in readiness and summoned the frontier chiefs to gather at Fort Beaufort, on the Kat River. At the resulting conference on 10 July, he then emphasised to those attending the pressing need for them to maintain their unity and sense of purpose. Dundas, meanwhile, warned the Boers to prepare for commando service. His period as civil commissioner was due to end on 1 July 1828, after which he was in fact under orders to rejoin his regiment, but on 25 June he received an instruction from General Bourke to assemble a small force, which he was then to lead on an intelligence-gathering expedition into Mpondoland itself, word having been received of a Zulu delegation at Faku's Great Place.[17]

With the news of Shaka's advance south, the Zulu embassy at Port Elizabeth was naturally seen in a more critical light, and Major A.J. Cloete was instructed to interview the Zulu chiefs further, being assisted in this task by Captain Evatt and Van der Riet. This time King was to be debarred from proceedings, to prevent him exercising any undue influence over the *izinDuna*. But this merely made Sothobe and Mbozamboza defensive and uncooperative. Not without reason, they felt they were being treated more like spies than high-ranking envoys and sought to return to their own country. Indeed, on 4 July, Mbozamboza escaped custody, and with one follower began the journey overland. Still in Zulu wardress they did not get far. Yet nothing was gained by the chiefs' continued retention, and on 2 August 1828, the Brig-sloop HMS *Helicon* entered the bay at Port Elizabeth in order to return the Zulu embassy to Natal. Even then the chiefs refused to board the ship without James Saunders King. The vessel reached Port Natal on 17 August.[18]

The Rev. Shrewsbury, writing from Butterworth on 30 June 1828, kept his elders (principally William Shaw) and brethren informed of developments. It is noticeable that in this context, he expressed himself in rather more emotional terms than in his communications with the colonial authorities. 'War', the reporting of which he described as 'painful and melancholy', 'is beginning to spread its Ravages amongst the natives of Southern Africa', he observed. He had seen the evidence of its imminence in his own region. On the very day (a Sabbath) that 'the Chapel was opened … successive companies of Caffres passed by, with their shields, and assagays, arrayed in

---

16 Cory, *Rise of South Africa*, II, p.355.
17 Peires, 'Matiwane's Road to Mbholompo', p.232.
18 J. Laband, *The Assassination of King Shaka* (Johannesburg: Jonathan Ball, 2017), pp.102–113; Cory, *Rise of South Africa*, II, p.356.

all the Panoply of War'. It was his understanding that the 'Chief Tshaka, or Chaka', was 'coming down the Coast, upon the Kaffers with immense Hordes of people under his command'. As far as he was aware, no general engagement 'has yet taken place'; 'but', he cautioned, 'Hintsa has resolved to fight, in a plain near the Bashe, about 34 miles from this [missionary] station'.[19]

The prospect filled Shrewsbury with dread. Shaka 'appears to be a Prince of unbounded ambition, and a monster of cruelty', he reported, with 'troops … drawn out in several divisions, distinguished by the colour of their shields'. When on the offensive 'one division goes forth to the fight', he asserted, 'and the others come to their aid, or reserve themselves for securing plunder, as circumstances may dictate'. Their sheer number and reputation was such that Shrewsbury feared for the very survival of what he called 'the Caffres', by which he meant primarily the Gcaleka under Hintsa. Already, '[w]ithin the last month', Shaka's forces had, he stated, 'routed and dispersed two Chiefs lying beyond us, and forced Dapa [Mdepa] to retire, so that nothing seems now to remain since the Tambookies and Mambookies have been overcome, but [for the Zulu] to fall on the Caffres [Xhosa] as quickly as possible'. By Tambookies and Mambookies, Shrewsbury meant the Thembu under Vusani (Ngubengcuka) and the Mpondo under Faku. Mdepa (in Hildegarde Fast's words, 'a minor chief of the Tshomane, an autonomous Mpondo chiefdom'), situated on the Umtata, was classed by Shrewsbury with the Mambookies.

Significantly, Mdepa was reputedly a descendant of a female European survivor of an unidentified shipwreck on the east coast of Africa in the mid eighteenth century (although not the *Grosvenor*, as Shrewsbury initially thought). This female European forebear had subsequently married a Tshomane chief, and for this reason Shrewsbury appears to have been particularly keen to cultivate a close connection with both the tribe and its mixed-race progeny. In response, the male descendant, Mdepa, was already purportedly requesting the placement of a mission station within his chiefdom. It was to result in the establishment in 1829, on the lower Umtata, of the Morley mission under William Shepstone – which, however, served to increase Mpondo–Tshomane tensions. This can hardly have been helped by Shrewsbury's belief that – Faku's father, Ngqungqushe, having been cruel towards 'the unfortunate crew of the Grosvenor' – God was 'visiting the iniquities of the Father … upon the son'.[20]

The alarm was real enough – William Shaw had himself visited Mdepa; while Shrewsbury, at Butterworth, described how he had been visited 'a few days ago' by some of Hintsa's 'counsellors', who 'asked if I would accompany them to the field of Battle, when the Enemy advances amongst them'. In response Shrewsbury explained that he must 'first provide for the safety' of his family, and that while 'I myself would stand by the Chief to the very last

---

19   WMS: MMS Box 301, 18: Shrewsbury to 'Honoured Father and Brethren', 30 June 1828, grammatically tidied in Fast (ed.), *Shrewsbury*, p.81.
20   WMS: MMS Box 301, 18: Shrewsbury to 'Father and Brethren', 30 June 1828; Fast (ed.), *Shrewsbury*, pp.60, 81–83, 190fn.115, 194fn.34, 198fn.116; T.J. Stapleton, *Faku: Rulership and Colonialism in the Mpondo Kingdom (c. 1760–1867)* (Waterloo, Ontario: Wilfrid Laurier University Press, 2001), pp.16, 35–41, 146, 165.

CONTROLLING THE FRONTIER

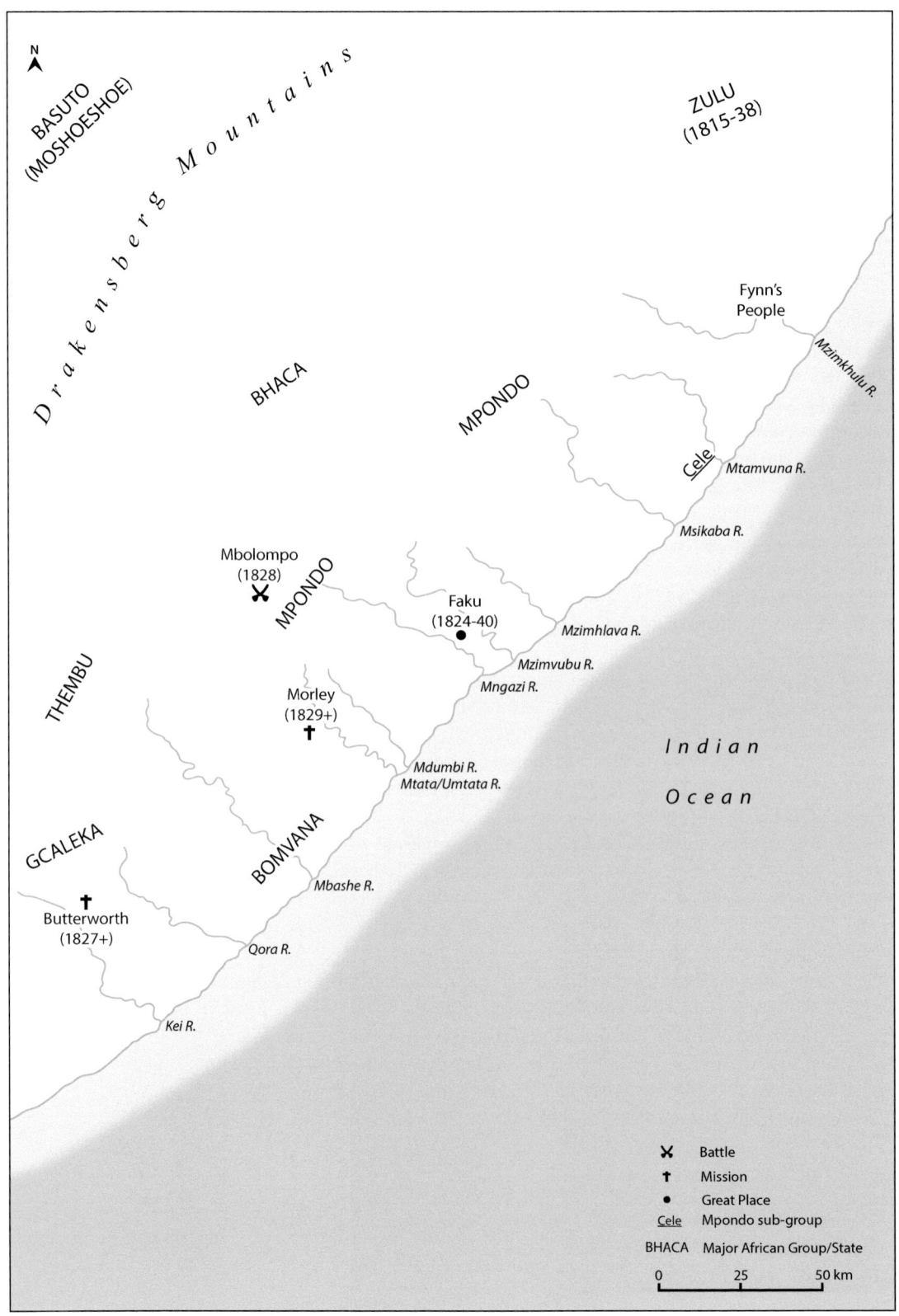

The Thembu and Mpondo kingdoms c.1820s.

extremity', he could not fight, 'for a missionary's hands must not be stained with blood'. Instead, he offered, 'if the Enemy would listen to arguments' and an interpreter would accompany him, to do all in his power 'to prevent the miseries of War' and promote peace.

At that moment Shrewsbury believed 'the Enemy' to be 'within 70 miles of Butterworth, and a little more than 20 of the place Hintsa designed to give him Battle'. That said, the Zulu there seemed 'content for the present' with securing the 'Booty' taken from Faku and with sending Hintsa 'a vaunting message' that he should 'take care that all the [Xhosa] Cattle were fat [for] when they "should come for them three months hence" [sic]'. But how much of this was reliable? In the same letter Shrewsbury also stated that '[l]ast year, Faku defeated a part of Chaka's forces, and slew his son', and that Shaka was at least in part motivated by revenge. There is no evidence for such an event (perhaps it was some garbled reference to the Zulu–Ngwane clash – to which we shall return – near what became Ladybrand, early in 1827), the report serving only to demonstrate the varying quality and reliability of much of the information being hurriedly gleaned from various frontier sources.[21]

There was also, of course, more than one area of focus, and as far as the situation facing the Thembu under Vusani (Ngubengcuka) was concerned, Shrewsbury, as would gradually emerge, was confusing the Zulu with the 'Fetcani' and, more particularly, the Ngwane. Thus there was still little clarity as to what forces were actually operating in the Transkei, or how they related to each other. In particular there was confusion as to whether certain raiding parties were 'Fetcani' or Zulu, or whether the two were connected; a confusion that was to find its way into subsequent reports. In a second letter to the frontier authorities, dated 2 July 1828, Shrewsbury wrote that on Sunday 29 June the Fetcani had 'completely routed and dispersed' Chief Faku of the Mpondo, who had retired towards Hintsa 'as far as the Umtata'; he then reported that Shaka 'now demands the heads of Hintsa and Vusani [Ngubengcuka]', the paramount chiefs of the Xhosa and Thembu respectively, and that consequently 'Vusani and Hintsa are preparing to make a firm stand against him on this side of the Bashee, but they fear being overpowered by numbers, the Fetcani being compared by the natives to locusts for numbers'. Shrewsbury here presents 'the Fetcani' and Zulu as effectively one and the same.

This would have been the sort of confused, if not conflicting, intelligence with which Major Dundas was supplied as he prepared to lead his small force into the territory beyond the Kei. Free of the constraints that as civil commissioner had led to his troubled relations with Colonel Somerset, Dundas assembled a unique commando consisting of 37 Boers drawn from the Winterberg district, together with a dozen volunteers from among the British settlers in Albany. These dozen settlers, most of whom had also responded to Major Dundas' call for volunteers during the Fetcani alarm of the previous year, were an enthusiastic 'band of brothers' – in some instances literally. They comprised Charles Theodore Bailie, the eldest son of John

---

21   WMS: MMS Box 301, 18: Shrewsbury to 'Father and Brethren', 30 June 1828; Fast (ed.), *Shrewsbury*, p.82.

CONTROLLING THE FRONTIER

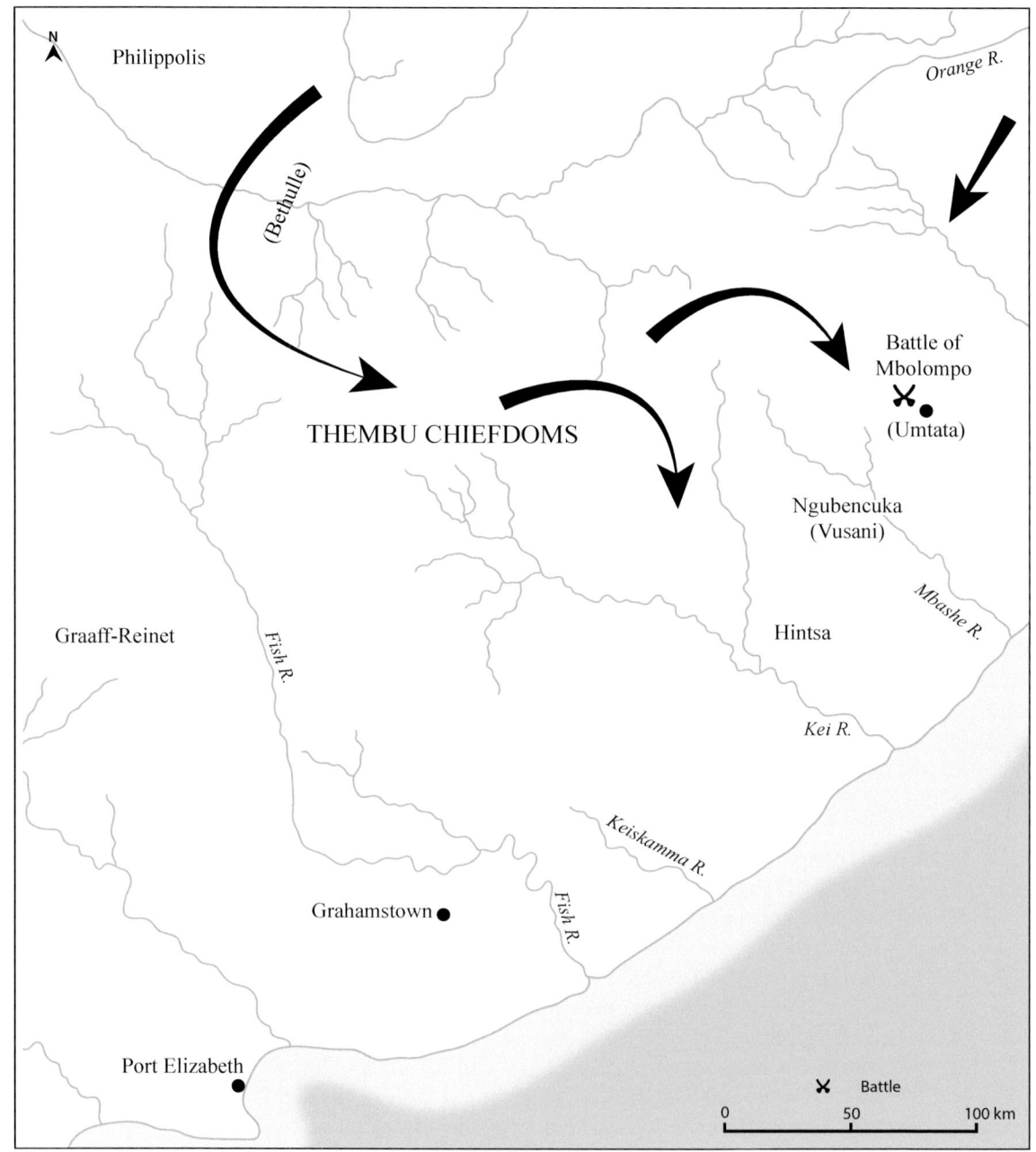

'Fetcani' raids 1825–1828.

Bailie: a renown young volunteer who ran the school and church at Bathurst, but who was subsequently to be killed during the Sixth Cape Frontier War after being led by Maqoma into an ambush at, of all places, Debe Nek (at the foot of Intaba-ka-Ndoda: that is, the site of the earlier Battle of Amalinde); J. Phillips; E. Phillips; W. Biddulph; T. Foxcroft; M. Cockcroft; Jas. and John Cawood (from the family who were soon to forge early trading links with Port Natal), and four brothers of the celebrated Bowker family who had adapted with great rapidity to frontier life: J.M., W.M., T.H. and B.E. Bowker. Bertram Egerton Bowker was to leave a written account of the expedition.[22]

Having first assembled the Dutch contingent of his commando at Kaffirs Drift, on the Fish River to the east of Bathurst, Dundas finally set off on 5 July 1828, making his way to the Rev. William Shaw's mission station at Wesleyville, a few miles beyond the Keiskamma River. It was there that the men from Lower Albany had been ordered to muster and meet him. Dundas, Bertram Bowker observed, 'had with him' two Khoikhoi soldiers, but he did not stand on ceremony. 'He used to buy a fat cow now and then when we wanted meat', he acknowledged, and in addition 'gave us beads and buttons to carry in our pockets, to buy milk and kaffircorn as we needed it'. 'Those', Bowker noted, 'were our rations'.[23]

From Wesleyville the party moved north to the Mount Coke mission station, before approaching the Kei River via Komgha, and then pushing on up to the Butterworth mission station itself, which was reached in good time on the evening of the third day of the journey from Kaffirs Drift. The intelligence gained there confirmed that both the Mpondos and, to their west, the Tambookies/Thembu had been driven from their lands, but as yet there was no reliable information as to where Shaka's army lay. Nonetheless, gathering a large number of mounted Galeka reinforcements from Hintsa, the commando continued its way to the Bashee River. William Shrewsbury accompanied Dundas for this stage of the journey, inadvertently causing further confusion to subsequent historians by in his diary identifying where they stopped as the Umtata.[24]

There was a halt of some days at the Bashee River, where defence measures were considered and supplies replenished. The most notable addition to the men's diet was hippopotamus meat, after what Bertram Bowker described as the 'splendid sport' of hunting two of these creatures, known at the time as 'seacows'. While hunting the men would generally use single or double-barrelled fowling pieces, which would fire buckshot for small game or round bullets for big game. Alternatively, they probably also carried an elephant gun. From these latest kills everyone had 'a jolly good feed', in addition to which plenty of meat was given 'to the Kaffirs', together with 'all the sjambok skins'. Bertram Bowker also described one of the improvised training sessions that Dundas initiated for what were again indiscriminately characterised as 'the Kaffirs'. He would 'put a hat on a stick 35 yards away', after which 'the first man to pierce the hat with his assegaai should have six buttons'. This challenge excited keen interest.[25]

---

22 Cory, *Rise of South Africa*, II, pp.348, 357; I. Mitford-Barberton, *Comdt. Holden Bowker: An 1820 Settler book including unpublished records of the Frontier Wars* (Cape Town & Pretoria: Human & Rousseau, 1970), pp.56-60.
23 Mitford-Barberton, *Bowker*, p.56.
24 '18 July 1828: Returned from the Umtata, whither I had accompanied Major Dundas, who has been sent by the British government to promise the Kafirs assistance against their common enemy, Chaka': Fast (ed.), *Shrewsbury*, p.83; Mitford-Barberton, *Bowker*, p.57; Cory, *Rise of South Africa*, II, p.358.
25 Mitford-Barberton, *Bowker*, p.57.

Following this extended stop, Major Dundas temporarily split his small command. Gathering together a group of the Albany volunteers, including the Bowker brothers, he left the remainder of the commando with Hintsa's forces and set out to find the Mpondos' paramount chief, Faku. Guides led the group to the site of Faku's Great Place, but the sight that met them served only to demonstrate the extent of the violence to which the location had been subjected. There was no one from whom to derive further information. The inhabitants had all fled -- but evidently not too long before, for domestic debris lay strewn over the ground and many of the burnt-out huts and cattle kraals were still smouldering.

When contact was finally made with Faku he clarified some of the immediate context. It was indeed the Zulu that had plundered the Mpondo kingdom, he was clear, and it had been continuing for a month and a half. It ended, as the colonial authorities understood it (subsequent oral testimony from the James Stuart Archive is varied and contradictory), with Faku accepting cattle from Shaka's emissaries – the Zulu delegation – in token either of Mpondo submission or some other manner of accommodation. In addition, Faku revealed that 'Henry Fynn and his small party' was 'with Chaka's army', subsequently confirming that the Mpondo had been attacked by 'Chaka's people, who had been accompanied by a party of armed Englishmen'. Fynn had been active among the Mpondo before, but what role Fynn's party (or other Port Natal traders) played in these immediate events – other than as an attachment to the Zulu campaign, as had been the case in similar instances at other times – has been disputed. Shaka, it is pertinent to note, had personally led his army as far south as the Mzimkhulu River, the eastern boundary of the Mpondo kingdom, where Fynn had already established what was ostensibly a trading base.[26]

Just how near hostile forces were soon became uncomfortably apparent. The Dundas group settled down for the night, intending to move on at first light. But at some time around midnight a regiment of hostile forces – Bertram Bowker was to identify it, rightly or wrongly, as a Zulu regiment 'under a chief named Natawana that had deserted from Dingaan' [*sic*] – began to pass close by. For a moment its war cry echoed from kraal to kraal, filling the vulnerable party of volunteers with terror. It may not have lasted long, but it was unsettling, for as Bowker wrote in his laconic notes, it sounded 'very war-like'. As soon as there was sufficient light to navigate the route, the scouting party made its way back to the Bashee defences.[27]

Once there, Dundas gathered his commando together and this time led it in a northerly direction, towards Tambookieland/Thembuland. Again there was soon evidence of widespread devastation, but with the grisly addition of numbers of decaying bodies – men, women and children – apparently the victims of recent raids. These raids had driven the paramount chief, Vusani (Ngubengcuka), deeper into the interior, while thousands of head of Tambookie cattle had simply been abandoned. Nonetheless, Dundas sought Vusani out and urged him to rally his people and strike back at the, as it

---

26   Peires, 'Matiwane's Road to Mbholompo', p.232; Stapleton, *Faku*, pp.19–21.
27   Cory, *Rise of South Africa*, II, p.358; Mitford-Barberton, *Bowker*, p.57.

was supposed, Zulu raiders. The appeal was superficially successful, but at a more uncertain level than Dundas evidently (initially at least) realised. A force, estimated to be as large as 6,000 strong (some 2,000 being under the sub-chief, Fobo), was assembled over a period of days and then directed east, towards the Umtata River, where the invaders were at length located.[28]

Dundas declined in any sense to compel, or attempt to compel, any member of the commando to participate in this undertaking. He was aware that, as Bertram Bowker put it, 'it was a very rough job', so reportedly gave each man the opportunity to stay behind. Or at least that was Bowker's understanding. In reality, as would soon become apparent, Dundas had no wish to participate in the expedition in any other role than, at best, adviser. Nonetheless, all the Albany volunteers agreed to go. But, perhaps on account of there being no discernible opportunity for subsequently securing women and children as servants, they were joined by only three of the Boers – and one of these quickly returned to camp with 'belly-ache'. Thus, if one includes Dundas himself, 15 members of the original commando went forward with the Tambookie/Thembu force. On the night of 25 July 1828, this force came to within sight of the enemy camp.[29]

At first light next morning, 26 July, the warriors amassed prior to attacking the camp, but by the time the chiefs, Vusani (Ngubengcuka) and Fobo, had delivered their traditional battlefield exhortations, if not indeed before, the enemy were aware that an attack was imminent and prepared to meet it. Led by the, to European eyes, bewildering sight of two shrieking witch doctors, the Tambookie/Thembu warriors advanced; however, while drawing as close as perhaps 100 yards, the adversaries held back from closing on each other. Instead, Vusani sent word to Major Dundas that his (Dundas's) men should loose off a volley with their weapons. Whether this request originated in some ill-defined or misunderstood battle plan (one certainly never communicated to the volunteers), meaning that the hiatus was to some extent calculated, or whether it was simply the outcome of fear or stemmed from some other cause (such as Dundas's disapproval of the line of attack, as he would later claim), cannot now be known for certain. However, the circumstantial evidence is not supportive of Dundas.

Dundas simply declined to fire, apparently indicating that it was for Vusani and the Tambookie to fight their own battle, particularly as the odds were stacked so heavily in their favour (an estimated 6,000, not including Hintsa's contingent, as against some 1,500 'Zulu'). This was an extraordinary stance to take. It was Dundas who had sought Vusani out and offered him – or at least led him to believe that he was gaining – assistance to repel the marauders. If he were now making some legalistic distinction between advising and fighting it would undoubtedly have been lost on Vusani, and was hardly the time to make it.

---

28 'Received a letter from Major Dundas', wrote William Shrewsbury in his diary on 23 July 1828, 'who recommended me to remove my family toward the Colony as the enemy was advancing and "the events of war are uncertain".' Fast (ed.), *Shrewsbury*, p.83.
29 Cory, *Rise of South Africa*, II, p.358; Mitford-Barberton, *Bowker*, p.58.

CONTROLLING THE FRONTIER

Thomas Philipps, influential and agitating 1820 Settler, who blamed Vusani (Ngubengcuka) for manipulating Major Dundas into the 'slaughter' of 'innocent individuals' on the Umtata. (Provenance unknown: reproduced as 'privately owned' in H.E. Hockly, *The Story of the British Settlers of 1820 in South Africa*, Cape Town: Juta & Co., 1948)

Dundas, in fact, previously appears to have been warned by Lieutenant Colonel John Bell, Secretary to the Cape Government, against becoming involved in any fighting, placing him in a most invidious position that now effectively unravelled.[30] Why then, Vusani may well have asked, had Dundas's men advanced there on the battlefield in company with his Thembu warriors? For as Bertram Bowker acknowledged: 'We were just on the right'. Nor did the stance hold. Still the warriors held back, and again Vusani urged Dundas to order his men to open fire. Dundas – who may have been concerned by the fact that the Albany volunteers had never before experienced battle – then responded by reluctantly ordering half the men only to do so; however, not even his own men could seemingly see the sense of that. Instead, they all fired. This appears to have been the origin of the report presently circulating in the eastern Cape that, in the words of the campaigning (and decidedly Whig) 1820 Settler, Thomas Philipps, 'Major D. was deceived by the Tambookie Chief Vasanie and suffered himself and a little retinue to be led by that Scoundrel [*sic*] to slaughter innocent individuals'.[31]

The enemy offered no serious resistance to this confused and not terribly effective initial attack. ('Only one man had his legs broken by our balls', admitted Bertram Bowker: 'We had bad guns in those days'.) Rather, they withdrew to a nek in the hills, where they were reinforced and from where they then had to be prised out by sharp, hand-to-hand fighting. Bertram Bowker and his fellow volunteers joined the attack. 'We galloped down through the Umtata river on the right', he recalled: 'On the next hill the Zulus had gathered in strength and turned again'. *Pace* Dundas's hesitations and Thomas Philipps's report, the Albany volunteers were by then anything but unwilling participants. It was, Bowker wrote, 'a splendid little fight … assegais striking shields … and us firing in from the right'. Indeed, far from being deceived into 'slaughter[ing] innocent individuals', the volunteers clearly had no compunction at all in this regard, Bowker recording how after the battle a 'few odd Zulus were shot, to chase them out from among the cattle'.[32]

This last engagement lasted some quarter of an hour, before the enemy again began to withdraw, eventually leaving Vusani (Ngubengcuka) in possession of anything between 10,000 (Bowker's estimate) to (Dundas's official estimate) 25,000 head of cattle. Bertram Bowker recorded 16 dead

---

30   Peires, 'Matiwane's Road to Mbholompo', p.232.
31   T. Philipps to Mrs Harries, 25 March 1829: Keppel-Jones (ed.), *Philipps*, p.350.
32   Mitford-Barberton, *Bowker*, p.59.

COLONIAL FORCES BEYOND THE FRONTIER: THE FETCANI ALARM

The fort aside, this detail from a contemporary *Illustrated London News* depiction of Xhosa removing their wounded and cattle from (in this case) Trompetter's Drift, provides a good indication of the scene that must have presented itself to Dundas as the Thembu withdrew in the wake of the confused Umtata engagement of 26 July 1828.

on the Tambookie side, 'and about the same number' among what he called 'the Zulu'. Dundas estimated '60 to 70 killed on the part of the enemy' ('no prisoners were taken', he added, not least perhaps because they were 'scattered over an extent of at least 12 square miles endeavouring to secure their cattle') for just one 'Tambooki'.[33]

There was little evidence of a fear of closing with the enemy in this latter attack, and after it Vusani was in no mood to have anything more to do with Major Dundas. The cattle were speedily rounded-up and driven off, accompanied by the rest of the Tambookie/Thembu force. Dundas and his men were left to their own devices, and soon found themselves in difficulties.[34]

There remained confusion about who precisely the enemy they had been opposing were. They certainly had not behaved like Shaka's warriors, and indeed they were not, although some of the young women previously held captive told Dundas that 'they were undoubtedly Chaka's people'.[35] But to label them as 'Fetcani' was little more than a confession of ignorance. In fact,

---

33 Dundas to Lieutenant Colonel Somerset, 1 August 1828: N.J. van Warmelo (ed.), *History of Matiwane and the amaNgwane Tribe as told by Msebenzi to his kinsman Albert Hlongwane, edited and supplemented by Archive Documents and other material by N.J. van Warmelo, Government Ethnologist* (Pretoria: Department of Native Affairs, 1938), p.240; Mitford-Barberton, *Bowker*, pp.59–60. Historian Julian Cobbing was to refer to 'the Thembu driving 'the awakening victims on to the British guns': 'The Mfecane as Alibi: Thoughts on Dithakong and Mbolompo', *Journal of African History*, 29 (1988), p.502. There is little basis for such a description: Peires, 'Matiwane's Road to Mbholompo', p.235.

34 Cory shows himself at his most unsympathetic to the black population in his account of these events. He is only too ready to ascribe cowardice and ingratitude to Vusani's (Ngubengcuka's) warriors, when no serious analysis can justify such crude and superficial judgements. Cory, *Rise of South Africa*, II, pp.358–360.

35 Dundas to Lieutenant Colonel Somerset, 1 August 1828: Van Warmelo, *History of Matiwane*, p.240. Dundas spoke of two 'Kaffer' (presumably Thembu) girls; Bowker wrote of how:

they were the accumulated remnant of the Ngwane tribe – the previously White Mfolozi-based tribe earlier identified by Mackay as marauding in Tambookieland/Thembuland – although even 'Ngwane' is something of a convenient catch-all label: Matiwane's following by then included numbers of Sotho, Tlokwa, Hlubi and other defeated peoples (there nonetheless remaining what Jeff Peires called 'an ethnic hierarchy' within the Ngwane regiments, with the Hlubi for example being regarded as 'servants').[36]

The Ngwane had originally been displaced from the White Mfolozi area as a result of attacks early in Shaka's reign, but they were still strong. Under Chief Matiwane they had then themselves attacked other tribes, such as the Amasizi (AmaZizi) – one of the tribes whose remnants would form the Fingo [*mfengu*: hungry/wandering] people (as indeed did elements of Matiwane's own Ngwane) and who were at that time living along the Tugela in Natal. Other sections of the Amasizi had submitted to Matiwane's authority and joined his force.[37] The Ngwane had then moved to the highveld in around 1822, where Matiwane reached the greatest extent of his power, defeating the Tlokwa and the Hlubi and compelling Moshoeshoe to pay him tribute.

Ngwane settlements had for some time been edging westward, to the point that by 1826 one of Chief Matiwane's outposts was only an estimated eight miles from Moshoeshoe's mountain stronghold of Thaba Bosiu. However, early in 1827 (around February), the Zulu crossed the Caledon and subjected the Ngwane to fresh attacks, a clash occurring more or less where the Free State town of Ladybrand would presently come to be established. The Ngwane would appear to have held their ground on that occasion (indeed, Shaka's half-brother, Dingane, reputedly received a wound to the chest during the engagement), but lost their cattle, leaving Matiwane only too aware of the ama-Ngwane's renewed vulnerability at the hands of an apparently resurgent Zulu.[38]

Matiwane began considering alternatives: a year later, in February 1828, the Ngwane dramatically (and on Matiwane's part, reluctantly) attacked Moshoeshoe and the Basuto, and it was at least partly the unexpected defeat they suffered (combined with raids from what were believed to be Shaka's Zulu again, but were later discovered to be Matabele marauders) that induced them to migrate east and south in mid 1828. It was a decision that led to some dissension within Ngwane ranks, centred on Matiwane's brother, Hawana; but the latter was defeated and killed, and the move went ahead – with disastrous consequences.[39]

Dundas and his men began to make their way back to the colony, but found themselves dangerously short of food and supplies. As soon became apparent, the Tambookie/Thembu were now far from inclined to help them

---

'Several young Kaffir women who had been captured by the Zulus joined us': Mitford-Barberton, *Bowker*, p.59.

36   Etherington, *Great Treks*, p.172; Peires, 'Matiwane's Road to Mbholompo', pp.214, 217, 234.
37   Cory, *Rise of South Africa*, II, p.359fn; Etherington, *Great Treks*, pp.130, 144fn.73.
38   Peires, 'Matiwane's Road to Mbholompo', p.219; Moloja quoted in D.F. Ellenberger, *History of the Basuto: Ancient and Modern* (London: Caxton Publishing Company, 1912), p.178.
39   P. Sanders, *Moshoeshoe, Chief of the Sotho* (London: Heinemann, 1975), pp.38–41; Peires, 'Matiwane's Road to Mbholompo', pp.220-221.

voluntarily. This was a serious matter because the 'Fetcani' troubles were in reality far from over. Far from at that stage fleeing or dispersing, the Ngwane in fact regrouped and consolidated, leaving both the Dundas commando and the Thembu in danger.

Evidence for this survives not only in Bowker's narrative, but also in the source entitled 'The Story of the "Fetcani Horde" by One of Themselves', first published in the *Cape Quarterly Review* in 1881/2. The narrator is one Moloja (Ellenberger spelt it 'Moloya'), 'a rank-and-file soldier of Matiwane' as Peires describes him, who had previously participated both in the battle against the Zulu on the Ladybrand site and then an extensive Ngwane reconnaissance into the Transkei region. Moloja subsequently settled in Basutoland, modern-day Lesotho, where he recounted his experiences to the long-lived government agent and sympathetic early historian of the Basuto, J.M. Orpen, who also published the narrative as a pamphlet, *The Story of the 'Fetcani Horde' by One of Themselves: Moloja, of Jozani's village, at Masite, near Morija, Basutoland* (Cape Town, 1882).[40]

Moloja related how Dundas and the Thembu force under Vusani (Ngubengcuka) had not in fact confronted the Ngwane forces under Matiwane in their entirety, 'only seven companies' or 'bands', as they were called, being engaged. The battle-hardened 'Ushee' or *uShiyi* regiment – of which Moloja was a member, and who had previously reputedly wounded Dingane – was left intact.[41] The recently captured cattle in Vusani's (Ngubengcuka's) possession were shortly to be driven off again in renewed attacks. Thus Dundas had ultimately succeeded in little more than alienating one of the colony's main allies in these continuing difficulties.

Nor had his expedition been properly coordinated with Colonel Henry Somerset's activities, no doubt in part because of the notorious inability of the pair to cooperate or communicate on anything but formal terms. Thus while Colonel Somerset at Fort Beaufort was in receipt of dispatches from Dundas up to shortly before the first clash on the Umtata, it was now far too late for Somerset to be able to provide effective short-term support.

Clashes on the Umtata: the Battle of Mbholompo

Nonetheless Colonel Somerset immediately prepared to take the field. He did so with some misgivings, fearing disturbances on the frontier in his absence. Nor was he alone. The missionaries at the Chumie and Lovedale stations sought military protection, and Lieutenant Ross was assigned the task. Ngqika had twice been summoned by Colonel Somerset, but had pointedly failed to respond and was suspected of hostile intentions. Indeed, the only

---

40 Peires, 'Matiwane's Road to Mbholompo', pp.215, 235; *Cape Quarterly Review*, 1, 2 (1881–1882), pp.267–217. A second printed version, containing some changes of wording, was incorporated into Ellenberger, *History of the Basuto*, pp.178–188. Ellenberger wrote in French; his son-in-law, J.C. Macgregor, then translated the text: DSAB III, pp.267–268.

41 Ellenberger, *History of the Basuto*, pp.178, 187–188; Peires, 'Matiwane's Road to Mbholompo', p.235.

losses to be suffered by the regular British army regiment with Somerset at this time, the 55th Foot, were to be among the understrength remnant left on the frontier. Two soldiers were murdered.

Colonel Somerset's regular force numbered about a thousand and consisted of a strong detachment of the 55th Foot (including the Grenadier company), under Lieutenant Colonel Mill; a detachment of the Royal Artillery, maintaining two ox-drawn six pounder guns, under Major Storey; and the newly formed 'Cape Mounted Riflemen'. But two commando units, under Commandants Durandt and Van Wyk, also accompanied the expedition. These Boers were drawn from the districts of Graaff-Reinet, Somerset, Uitenhage, and Albany, and numbered altogether 531. There were no British settlers among them.[42]

The 55th Foot had been in the colony for some years. Under the command of Lieutenant Colonel Skerrett, the headquarters and right wing of the regiment (as it was described in the regiment's digest of service) had embarked at Gravesend on the East Indiaman *Sir David Scott* on 8 December 1821; the left wing of the regiment under Major Mill having embarked on the 3rd on board the *Earl of Balcarras*. The *Earl of Balcarras* duly arrived at Table Bay on 26 February, but the four companies aboard were only finally disembarked on 2 March at Robben Island, where they had to undergo a quarantine of three weeks on account of the 'measles' that had, it was said, 'made its appearance in the ship during the passage'. By the time the men were finally brought over to Cape Town they were able immediately to join the 'Head Quarter Division', which had arrived in Table Bay on 13 March and disembarked the following day. On 3 November 1823, the command of the regiment then devolved upon Major Mill, Lieutenant Colonel Skerrett having obtained leave to return to England.

On 14 July 1824, one company of the 55th proceeded to what was still described as Algoa Bay, followed exactly a month later by another company with orders to proceed to Grahamstown. However, the following year saw something of an interruption to this period of service when the regiment was officially extended to its full six service and four depot companies, and Major Mill led a mission back to the regimental depot at Carlisle to oversee the expansion. He was promoted lieutenant colonel and assumed command of the regiment on his arrival. Major Brock was left in command of the service companies at the Cape.

Shortly after, the service companies were officially transferred to the eastern frontier. Two hundred and forty five NCOs and other ranks embarked at Simon's Bay on board the naval frigate *Owen Glendower* on 13 September 1827. They disembarked at Port Elizabeth on the 18th and, in the words of the regimental digest, 'marching from thence reached Graham's Town on the 23rd, the remainder under Captain Frend coming up soon afterwards'. Once there, the men were dispersed in the usual manner, as was succinctly logged: 'The Head Quarters with the two Flank Companies continued at Graham's

---

42 P.J. Young, *Boot and Saddle: A Narrative Record of the Cape Regiment, the British Cape Mounted Riflemen, the Frontier Armed Mounted Police, and the Colonial Cape Mounted Riflemen* (Cape Town: Maskew Miller, 1955), p.17; Cory, *Rise of South Africa*, II, p.360.

Town, the other companies being detached at Algoa Bay and along a line of Posts on the North-East Frontier of the Colony'.[43]

By the time of Colonel Somerset's 'expedition to the interior' the regiment had thus been stationed on the eastern frontier a little under a year, having arrived shortly after the Fetcani alarm of 1827 had subsided. With the onset of a renewed Fetcani/Zulu crisis in June 1828, the regiment was ordered to Fort Beaufort where, the digest records, it was joined 'by most of the Detachments'. In other words, the Grahamstown contingent marched to Fort Beaufort, where it met up with its detached companies previously stationed along the line of frontier posts, and where the regiment was also to find assembled the 'Cape Mounted Rifle Corps … a Detachment of Artillery and a force of armed Burghers'.

Having set out on 25 July, the expeditionary force reached the Kei River on 31 July 1828. But due to the continuing lack of reliable intelligence concerning 'Zulu' movements and intentions, it was to remain there for nearly three weeks. It was an uncomfortable interlude. Apart from the uncertainty, it was cold, there was considerable rainfall, and provisions were already becoming scarce. Indeed, on the first night after making camp a thunderstorm caused such pandemonium that a number of transport oxen were killed and some 50 horses succeeded in breaking free of their picket ropes and stampeding into the darkness. Parties of Cape Mounted Riflemen were presently sent after them, and two days were spent in the pursuit.[44]

Late on the evening of 2 August 1828, William Shrewsbury noted in his diary, 'two officers' arrived at the Butterworth mission station from 'the British camp' to inform him of these latest developments and gain further intelligence. '[I]t seems the Colonial government have thought proper to send out a strong force of military with about 800 [sic] Boors under Lieutenant Colonel Somerset to check the Fikanes', he observed – the language and over estimation of the number of Boers suggesting that he was not wholly approving of, or comfortable with, its composition. Nonetheless, it 'may end well', he thought, for (as Shrewsbury had presumably been advised by the officers) 'Hintsa received certain information today that Major Dundas had only routed those of the enemy who were in advance, but that the main body had since come up under one of the chief warriors, with a full resolution to conquer and take full possession of Kafirland'.[45]

On 11 August, Shrewsbury apparently received confirmation of this via a messenger or messengers sent directly from Hintsa himself. 'This morning Hintsa sent to inform us that Chaka is still bent on war and bringing on a vast body of people', he noted in his diary. According to Shrewsbury, Hintsa – now in alliance with Somerset's force – professed himself to be more 'exasperated than intimidated by his late defeat, and resolved to put forth his utmost power to drive all before him'.[46]

---

43 Regimental Museum of The Border Regiment and The King's Own Royal Border Regiment: 55th Foot, Digest of Service (unpubl. MS).
44 Young, *Boot and Saddle*, p.17.
45 Fast (ed.), *Shrewsbury*, p.84.
46 Fast (ed.), *Shrewsbury*, pp.84–85.

From all sides events appeared to be moving towards a resolution, in which Shrewsbury naturally purported to see the hand of God. Thus on the morning of 14 August, as Shrewsbury recorded, 'Lieutenant Colonel Somerset arrived [at Butterworth] … with a party of troops', while 'more came in [over] the following days, besides a considerable number of the Dutch farmers'. Their aim, in Shrewsbury's words, was specifically (or at least first and foremost) 'to oppose Chaka's people who are still advancing on the Kafirs', and his diary gives no reason to doubt that this was indeed (as they understood it) the case. Were it not so there would presumably have had to have been a concerted dissembling for Shrewsbury's benefit, which seems unlikely.[47]

Sunday, 17 August 1828, saw the mixed force gather for divine service. Shrewsbury was gratified at what he witnessed. 'Congregation this afternoon was very large', he noted, 'the chapel not being able to contain the mingled assembly of English, Dutch and Kafirs [that is, Khoikhoi, the Cape Mounted Riflemen], to whom I preached.' All, he believed, heard his words 'with deep and serious attention'. He was impressed. 'The Sabbath', he ventured, 'has been sanctified by the British beyond what I had expected to have seen, under their circumstances.' The circumstances were that the force was under notice to march next day.[48]

Vusani (Ngubengcuka) and Hintsa, with whom Somerset clearly retained good (if not always reliable) communications, had seemingly not only identified the enemy as being somewhere on the left bank on the Bashee, but also of being desirous of effecting a meeting with (in Cory's words) 'the white men who assisted the Tambookies [Thembu]'. Therefore on Monday, 18 August 1828, the expeditionary force moved on through a bare, broken, unyielding landscape that continued to take its toll on horses and oxen alike. On 22 August it arrived at the river, but in the event no enemy encampment or outpost was found. Vusani and Hintsa, meanwhile, had gathered their forces at a rendezvous point some five miles distant.[49]

Colonel Somerset moved on to join them, with unverified reports and rumours of the – as it was still believed – Zulu enemy supposedly still being as close by. Somerset would later imply that these movements of the enemy constituted an immediate threat to his force. In view of subsequent events, that would seem unlikely, but enemy scouting or reconnaissance parties were doubtless observed and promptly followed up. Served by up-to-date intelligence reports (but still under a misapprehension as to who precisely the enemy were), Colonel Somerset directed his collected forces to move forward in a guarded reconnaissance sweep.

In a short time an enemy encampment was identified. As Somerset later reported it, 'at 2 p.m. on the 26th [August] the Chiefs Hynsa and Vousanie sent expresses to me to inform me that the enemy was advancing in great force upon the plain about six miles from my position and that they [Hintsa and Vusani] had consequently moved their armies up the hill, and they begged I would lose no time in joining them from Beechy' (that is, the River

---

47   Fast (ed.), *Shrewsbury*, p.85.
48   Fast (ed.), *Shrewsbury*, p.85.
49   Cory, *Rise of South Africa*, II, p.361.

Bhityi). In other words, in his official despatch Somerset would later accord the initiative for this final advance to his native allies, suggesting that he was anxious to diffuse responsibility for what ensued ('I lost no time in moving forward with my division', he stated). The march to contact commenced at dusk on 26 August 1828 and continued until one in the morning, when the warriors, soldiers and Boers rested on the near side of a hill situated above the Umtata River. The native allies were by then an estimated 16,000 strong, with 'the armies of each Chief being in separate columns'. The enemy was encamped at various points on the far side, in a vale known as Mbholompo. This was mountainous country some miles west of the present-day town of Umtata. On older or more detailed maps a 'Matuana Mountain' is situated there (the village of Lugxogxo, where the battle is commemorated, lies some 19 miles west of Umtata). Three hours later, as daylight approached, the climb was continued to a point a little below the crest of the hill, thus leaving the strength of this force hidden from enemy view.

At some time after 4:00 a.m., with the first glimpse of daylight, Colonel Somerset reportedly sent one of his best officers, Captain Robert Scott Aitchison (sometimes spelt Aitcheson, previously an officer in the Cape Corps, having joined in 1819, and later a witness before the far-reaching Parliamentary Select Committee on Aborigines), together with an interpreter and a 20 man escort, over the crest with the aim of opening a dialogue with the enemy, in the apparent belief that they were part of Shaka's army. That at least was the official position. But given that it was barely dawn and the settlement was apparently largely asleep, can it be true? The Wesleyan missionary, Stephen Kay (to whom we shall return), thought not, and subsequently stated that 'the unanimous testimony ... is altogether against this assertion, showing too clearly, that time was not allowed for anything of the kind'.[50]

On the other hand, as Somerset indeed indicated, there would presumably have been some kind of guard or picket; and given that they were not in fact Zulus, but in reality Matiwane's Ngwane again, who would hardly see in such moves anything but a threat, it is not wholly inconceivable that, as Colonel Somerset watched from a distance, enemy warriors moved as if to surround the members of Aitchison's approaching party and then, as feared, attempted to rush them before any dialogue could be successfully initiated. Moreover, were it otherwise, it would seem odd that Captain Aitchison should not have objected to his name being cited in this manner. 'The manner in which the Mounted Rifle Corps was led into action by Captain Aitchison' reflected the highest credit on the Corps, Somerset subsequently recorded. For immediately (as it was stated) his party fled for their lives, while simultaneously Colonel Somerset ordered his regular troops to go to their aid.

---

50   Somerset to Major General Bourke, 'Bashee River, 29 August 1828': Van Warmelo, *History of Matiwane*, pp.252-253; S. Kay, *Travels and Researches in Caffraria: Describing the Character, Customs, and Moral Condition of the Tribes inhabiting that Portion of Southern Africa: with Historical and Topographical Remarks Illustrative of the State and Prospects of the British Settlement in its Borders, and the Introduction of Christianity, and the Progress of Civilization* (London: John Mason, 1833), p.330.

CONTROLLING THE FRONTIER

No illustrations survive of the Battle of Mbholompo, but the manner of fighting experienced is well captured in this later depiction of 'A skirmish in the Open' during the 1850-53 Frontier War. (Lithograph from Lucas, *Pen and Pencil Reminiscences of a Campaign in South Africa*)

In any event, contrivance or otherwise, it was from this initial 'defensive' fighting that a general action ensued. Aitchison and his interpreter were in the most danger as they were furthest forward, and indeed the latter's tunic was cut open in the mêlée; but they both survived. However, although the fighting quickly spread and became general, the native allies in Somerset's force allegedly initially refrained from becoming involved, holding to their position on the crest of the ridge. Only when the engagement was clearly going against the enemy did they, as it appeared, join the fray, and then it was primarily in order to attack and kill the women, children, and other camp followers – a practice to which, as soon as the situation allowed, Colonel Somerset was adamant he put a stop.

Or again, that was the official position. Almost certainly some such killing occurred, but equally it was politically expedient to place most responsibility for it on 'the Kaffers', and Colonel Henry Somerset was just the sort of man to do so. If he did, as seems likely, put a stop to such killing, it was not least because he and the Boers wanted to take these women and children alive for their own purposes.[51]

---

51   Jeff Peires: 'I have had previous experience with Colonel Henry Somerset's lying and self-serving dispatches': 'Matiwane's Road to Mbholompo', p.236. In his report Somerset also states that at some point 'the army of the Kaffers' was reinforced by 'several thousand men under Fakoo', bringing their collective total to some 26,000: Somerset to Major General Bourke, 29August 1828: Van Warmelo, *History of Matiwane*, p.253. But while there may

This further example of a lack of coordination between largely European and colonial troops and their recent and, it was only too evident, merely expedient native allies, had little effect on the outcome of the battle. It was a triumph of the gun over the assegai and shield – and not least a 'triumph', if that is the word, of the field gun. The employment of the two six pounders in such a constricted environment was no easy matter, as Somerset acknowledged, and the manner in which they were successfully brought into action was – from a purely operational perspective – a credit to the small, well trained, artillery detachment. 'From the great difficulty that occurred in bringing up the guns drawn by oxen, I was not able to get [them] into action so early as I wished', Somerset reported to General Bourke: 'Major Storey was however able towards the close of the action to throw several shots with some effect'. They did indeed have 'some effect' for, however limited by European standards, the bombardment had a deep psychological effect on the Ngwane, who had never before experienced such armaments. 'We knew not then what it was', Moloja related; 'we heard a terrific noise, and saw fire and smoke, and deadly burning things pierced and killed us where we stood.'[52] Reports of the astonishing effectiveness of these weapons were carried far and wide with the chaotic dispersal of Matiwane's people. So much so that when Mzilikazi of the Matabele first met the missionary Robert Moffat a little over a year later, he was reported to have said that he wanted 'a large gun' with which he too could destroy his enemies 'before they even came in sight', having heard of such 'from the Fikani'.[53]

There was no reported loss of life among regular or colonial forces, and no record of the loss of life among their opponents – although it cannot have been small, for the fighting was said to have lasted for well over seven hours and was at times fierce. Colonel Somerset, in the clipped, measured tones of an official dispatch, attempted to emphasise (perhaps overemphasise) the fury apparently unwittingly unleashed. Nothing could exceed 'the determined and daring conduct of the enemy', he recorded, but such was the nature of the engagement that it was impossible to ascertain numbers. 'As well as I am able to judge I estimate their force at about twenty thousand, but as they continued receiving large reinforcements from the other side of the mountain, I cannot give a very accurate idea of it.' 'They made constant and continued attempts to charge my forces', he went on, 'and appeared determined neither to give nor receive quarter', for which they must have paid a heavy price in blood. Finally '[a]fter a continued fire from six o'clock to about half past one, the enemy was driven from all

---

have been some direct Mpondo involvement, it appears to have been piecemeal and marginal; Vusani (Ngubengcuka) subsequently married Faku's daughter, Nonesi, but it did not end Thembu–Mpondo hostility over the following decade. See William B. Boyce, *Notes on South African Affairs, From 1834 to 1838; with Reference to the Civil, Political, and Religious Condition of the Colonists and Aborigines* (Graham's Town: Aldum & Harvey, 1838/Cape Town: Struik, facs. reprint, 1971), p.115; and Stapleton, *Faku*, pp.22-23.

52   Somerset to Major General Bourke, 29 August 1828: Van Warmelo, *History of Matiwane*, p.256; Ellenberger, *History of the Basuto*, p.188.

53   J.P.R. Wallis (ed.), *The Matabele Journals of Robert Moffat*, I, pp.27–28, quoted in Etherington, *Great Treks*, p.173.

points and retired up the mountain.' For this, he praised in particular the 'Burghers under Field Commandant Durandt' whom, he placed on record, had 'behaved in the most gallant and determined manner' (by that time he adjudged the burghers under Durandt to be 120 strong and those under van Wyk 'about' 100 in number); but he also drew attention to the conduct of the 'Flank Companies of the 55th', under Lieutenant Colonel Mill, and what he called 'the Civil Hottentots' under the command of Lieutenant Sinclair ('who has commanded this Corps since the army took the field'), who between them successfully 'drew the enemy from all their positions on the left face of the mountain'. [54]

Recriminations followed the victory. As a result of their warriors' behaviour Colonel Somerset informed both Vusani (Ngubengcuka) and Hintsa that they had forfeited any entitlement to military assistance from the colony. But it is evident that neither of the chiefs regarded this assistance as anything to be relied upon, nor necessarily in their own interests. The colonial government had intervened for its own political ends. Nor were denunciations of the killing of enemy women and children likely to have much effect.

On the other hand the aftermath allegedly left Colonel Somerset with something of a dilemma, namely what to do with the survivors of the Thembu/Gcaleka inflicted massacre of women and children, and also such widows and orphans of the main battle that remained – or rather, how to account for them, for there was little doubt as to how they would be accommodated. The acquisition of cattle and child servants had long been standard practice among Boers called out on commando, and it was a practice to which Colonel Somerset was prepared to give a nod and a wink. Officially as many as 47 women and 70 children remained under the protection of the colonial forces. There may well have been more. 'Colonel Somerset', wrote Cory disingenuously, 'was at a loss to know what to do with them as they refused to go back to their own people.' At which point, '[s]ome of the Boers offered to take care of them until they reached the Colony'. 'This was approved', Cory continued, as if noting an unexpected philanthropic gesture, 'and Field-Commandant Durand [sic] made a list of them which was eventually handed to the Civil Commissioner of Albany and Somerset', Captain Duncan Campbell.[55]

Given the well known (and subsequently open) propensity of the Boers for capturing children on commando to become servants, this aspect of the expedition merits further investigation, but in general prisoners taken by regular troops in the course of the battle do not seem to have been mistreated. Within a year of their capture they were, in Peires's words, 'free inhabitants of the Transkei [that is, Xhosa] region'.[56] It was largely from these survivors that it was learnt that the opposing force was not Shaka's,

---

54   Somerset to Major General Bourke, 29 August 1828: Van Warmelo, *History of Matiwane*, p.256; Cory, *Rise of South Africa*, II, p.362.
55   Cory, *Rise of South Africa*, II, pp.362–363; Somerset to Major General Bourke, 29 August 1828: Van Warmelo, *History of Matiwane*, p.255.
56   Peires, 'Matiwane's Road to Mbholompo', p.223.

but Matiwane's; they were the Ngwane again. Shaka's forces were by that time withdrawing north.

Matiwane was now decisively defeated and fled. For some time he wandered through the territory of his old adversary, Moshoeshoe, whom he had attempted to defeat only some six months before. Moshoeshoe characteristically even offered him sanctuary.[57] However, Matiwane was seemingly intent on returning to his former homeland on the Tugela.

He reached the area in the wake of Shaka's assassination and, after presenting himself as a suppliant to Dingane, was eventually executed by order of the new King – his place of execution close by uMgungundlovu thereafter becoming known as kwaMatiwane (subsequently the scene of the murder of Piet Retief and his men). According to legend, before ordering Matiwane's death, Dingane had 'bared his breast, and pointing to the scar of the wound … received at Ladybrand', said very gently: 'Knowest thou that wound?'[58]

Andries Pretorius and the Voortrekkers' 'Cattle Commando' (*Beeskommando*) would encounter the remnant of the Ngwane tribe on the Tugela a little over a decade later. At that time (January 1840) the Ngwane were domiciled in the hills to the north of present day Ladysmith and Matiwane's son, Zikhali, was leading them. Nonetheless Zikhali was evidently still known, or referred to, by the name of his late father, the Voortrekkers giving his name as 'Mattowan' and the accompanying French naturalist, Adulphe Delegorgue, rendering it as 'Matouana'. Zikhali offered to assist Pretorius in the Voortrekkers' war against Dingane, seeking in return a grant of land on which to live – an offer that was provisionally accepted. However, Zikhali was subsequently accused of pilfering significant numbers of captured Zulu cattle and in addition murdering and maiming Mantatese/Tlokwa living under the troublesome chief, Witsi. He was taken as a prisoner to Pietermaritzburg, but thereafter released. A survivor, sometime later also nearly clashed with the Hlubi led by Langalibalele, but ultimately the Hlubi and Ngwane lived in peace on the slopes of the Drakensberg range, 'in the shadow of Champagne Castle and Cathedral Peak'.[59]

Colonel Somerset, meanwhile, reaped little benefit from the victory, for the Mbholompo campaign increasingly became the cause of bitter and partisan dispute. Thus the prominent campaigner, Saxe Bannister, author of *Humane Policy; or Justice to the Aborigines of New Settlements*, published in London in 1830, who was in the colony during this period, would refer darkly to 'the bloody events of 1828'. But most influential of all was the Wesleyan missionary, Stephen Kay, who placed the most damning construction upon these events in his book, *Travels and Researches in Caffraria*, published in 1833.

Kay's views were to carry considerable weight in philanthropic circles. He quoted an unnamed 'respectable British officer' as subsequently describing the engagement succinctly as 'one of the most disgraceful and cold-blooded

---

57   Matiwane reputedly answered: 'No; I can be killed by a chief, but not by a servant'. Ellenberger, *History of the Basuto*, pp.188-189.
58   J.C. Macgregor in Ellenberger, *History of the Basuto*, p.189.
59   Liebenberg, *Pretorius*, pp.109, 130–131, 133; Etherington, *Great Treks*, pp.286–287.

WMS missionary, Stephen Kay, who denounced the events at Mbholompo. (National Library of South Africa, Cape Town)

acts to which the English soldier had been accessory', with Kay (if not the unnamed and partially quoted officer) implying that the regular troops were directly party to the admitted Thembu/Gcaleka massacre of women and children. The 'military force' had been 'joined by an immense host of Kaffers, who proved themselves to be Kaffers indeed!' Kay wrote, in a generally unquoted passage. Indeed, as Kay depicted it the whole event was not a battle at all, but rather a premeditated and undiscriminating massacre. 'The moment our troops arrived on the summit of the eminence that overlooked the vale in which Matuwana and his men were lying', he affirmed, 'orders were given for all to gallop down amongst the houses. Their affrighted occupants then poured out in droves, and a dreadfully destructive fire was forthwith opened upon them.' No pity was shown. 'Numbers, gaunt and emaciated by hunger and age, crawled out of their miserable sheds, but with pitiable apathy sat or laid down, as if heedless of their fate.' 'Who can conceive of a situation more awful?' he asked rhetorically. 'The thought of it makes one's blood run cold.'

And yet Kay concedes that the Ngwane 'were armed in a moment', regrouped and fought 'bravely', until the field guns broke their protracted resistance.[60] Nor was Kay's a universally accepted interpretation of events, even among the missionaries themselves. Kay's fellow Wesleyan, William Boyce, the resident missionary at Butterworth, was to speak just as forcefully of 'the humanity of [the] British interference in 1828', and in years to come he continued to maintain that the intervention had been both just and politic. Thus in *Notes on South African Affairs*, published in 1838 (in the wake of the Sixth Cape Frontier War), Boyce reiterated his view that the 'establishment of regular official communications, between the Colonial Government and the Tambookie and Amapondo Chiefs, Vadanna and Faku, would tend to give the executive a commanding influence on the frontier'. These chiefs had, he stated, 'uniformly manifested a friendly disposition [to the colonial government, not to each other], which has been tested by trying and difficult circumstances', and they remained potentially important allies. 'If the good offices of the Colonial Government were employed for the preservation of peace between these chiefs, and a frequent communication were kept up',

---

60 S. Kay, *Travels and Researches in Caffraria*, pp.330–331; S. Bannister, *Humane Policy; or Justice to the Aborigines of New Settlements, Essential to a Due Expenditure of British Money, and to the Best Interests of the Settlers, with suggestions how to Civilise the Natives by an Improved Administration of Existing Means* (London: Thomas & George Underwood, 1830), p.150ff; Cory, *Rise of South Africa*, II, pp.363–364; DSAB I, p.50; IV, pp.270–271.

COLONIAL FORCES BEYOND THE FRONTIER: THE FETCANI ALARM

Boyce argued, 'the effect would be most beneficial in convincing the border Kaffers [that is, the Xhosa] of the necessity of remaining at peace with the colony, which had secured such powerful friends in the rear.'

Look at Europe, he urged, in an interesting but perhaps questionable parallel: 'By thus maintaining the balance of power in Europe, many aggressions are prevented, and there is no reason why a similar line of policy in South Africa should not be attended with equal success'. Boyce was in some ways prescient. Just some two years after that statement, through the actions of the Voortrekkers in Natal, Faku would (through Wesleyan missionary intermediaries) ask the British authorities to bring the Mpondo kingdom under its protection. As a result, the then Governor of the Cape, Sir George Napier, would dispatch a small force under Captain Thomas Charlton Smith. It was a development with far-reaching consequences for the region.[61]

However, notwithstanding any of this, Andries Stockenström accepted Kay's denouncements without reservation, and was indeed to cite Kay when referring to these matters in his autobiography.

From Stockenström's account one would hardly be aware that the Ngwane were involved in marauding. Indeed, he appears no more certain in retrospect than Colonel Somerset was at the time who the opponents actually were, referring to them in a not very well informed tirade – aimed in large measure at the Somersets – as 'Fetcani'. Major Dundas's commando, he reported, had opened fire on perceiving an attempt by their opponents to surround them, and the 'Fetcani' had then moved away in the hope of settling down 'in the open uninhabited country about the sources of the Umtata'. There they were innocently massacred. All was peaceful when

WMS missionary, William Boyce, who supported the intervention. (National Library of South Africa, Cape Town)

> one morning at break of day an Anglo-Galeka army, under Colonel Somerset, fell upon them unexpectedly with great guns, and small guns, and sabres and assagais, and made such indiscriminate havoc before the savages were awake, or knew what had come upon them, that the panic was so complete that our Kaffir allies had only to complete the *victory* [sic] by atrocities such as exaggeration has hardly been able to lay to the charge of that monster Nana Sahib.

---

61 Boyce, *Notes on South African Affairs*, pp.115–116; Cory, *Rise of South Africa*, II, p.364; Liebenberg, *Pretorius*, pp.222–224; Stapleton, *Faku*, pp.56–59.

CONTROLLING THE FRONTIER

The implication is that the native allies were set on their course of killing women and children – Nana Sahib was reviled above all for ordering the massacre of women and children at Cawnpore during the Indian Mutiny – by Colonel Somerset's indiscriminate and unprovoked attack. Stockenström's bitterness seeps through his account, for he was apparently told at the time that any investigation of the case was 'exclusively military' and therefore not his responsibility. He quotes an exchange with an officer in which, by his own account, he lost his temper and set off on something of a rant about doing his duty 'in defiance of uncles or fathers', and how 'a wholesome fear of the Horse Guards and its Secretary' paralysed his contemporaries. 'It is to me perfectly clear that no Civil Governor will ever be able to control the Frontier, with Colonel Somerset as Commandant and his uncle [Lord Fitzroy Somerset, later Lord Raglan] omnipotent at Head Quarters', he was said to have raged. This does not suggest someone looking at the issue impartially, but it is the account most often quoted by historians.[62]

Much of this subsequent controversy would no doubt have astonished the 55th Foot. In the regimental digest no mention is made of Gcaleka/Thembu involvement. But neither does it describe the engagement as much of a battle. Instead it simply records that the force of which it was a part, 'arriving on the morning of the 27th August on the banks of the Umtata drove back a tribe of savages under their chief Matuana who had been endeavouring to dispossess the Tambookie Caffres of their country and cattle'. That it was an unpleasant affair cannot be doubted. 'This service performed', the digest concluded without lingering, 'the corps returned to their respective quarters (,) the Head Quarters reaching Graham's Town on the 14th September.'

Letters of Private George Witcherley

Internecine violence among the tribes beyond the frontier was, it appeared to the ordinary soldier, endemic in the general unrest following on Shaka's advance south – and it was, of course, with a section of Shaka's army that they initially thought they were confronted. It is unlikely that they would have seen themselves as having been involved (except perhaps indirectly) in 'one of the most disgraceful and cold-blooded acts to which the English soldier had been accessory', although it is not impossible that the 'respectable British officer' cited by Kay was a member of the 55th Foot. This general attitude is well illustrated in the correspondence of a private soldier of the regiment, which has survived the vagaries of the years.

Born in 1800, George Witcherley (which name he spelt inconsistently, although he had clearly benefitted from a degree of education, displaying neat handwriting) came from Market Drayton and enlisted in the 55th Foot at Shrewsbury in March 1820. Three letters from southern Africa survive, addressed to his mother and father. The first, written from the 'Cape of Good Hope', has an indecipherable date, but mentions his belonging to

---

62   Hutton (ed.), *Stockenström*, I, pp.279–281; Mostert, *Frontiers*, pp.604–605. Etherington relates the action in similar terms: *Great Treks*, pp.172–173.

COLONIAL FORCES BEYOND THE FRONTIER: THE FETCANI ALARM

Grahamstown, as Private George Witcherley of the 55th Foot would have known it in 1828. The first church was completed in 1830. (Cory, *Rise of South Africa* II, 'from a water-colour sketch by Dr. W.G. Atherstone, 1833, redrawn by F.W. Armstrong, Esq.')

Captain Sumbley's Company and in addition asks his father to 'let James Whittiker's friends know that he [Whittiker] is safe … at Simons Bay … with his Company'.[63] In the next letter, dated 'Grahames town 14 January 1828', he explains that he is batman or orderly to one of the regiment's officers. 'I have been living with a Captain of my Regiment As [sic] a servant for this 2 years and a ½', he states, having been engaged in the 'same situation' or a 'like station' since 'I left my tender mother and father'. He then outlined something of his current posting.

'I left Cape Town on 13th September [1827] and marched for Grahams town', he tells his father, conceding that it was 'a long and fatiguing march'. 'This [that is, the Grahamstown district] is called the front tiere of Africa', he noted, but there was clearly an underlying fear of potential, if not yet prospective, instability, for men of the regiment were even then being posted in a thin defensive arc as much as a hundred miles from the settlement. It was, Witcherley thought, 'the worst Part of the world' to which English soldiers were sent, his understanding (as presumably among the regiment more widely) being that they were defending the vulnerable frontier Africans – Witcherley, indeed, telling his family that '[there] [is] a[n] African tribe come Down upon tham [them], and the [Governor?] Had to [send?] the 55 Regiment to their assistance'.

He saw the purpose; nonetheless, he found it difficult to accommodate himself to the environment or, notwithstanding his religious sensibilities (shades of Rev. Shrewsbury's 'divine service' on Sunday 17 August), summon much sympathy for, or empathy with, the indigenous population. 'I found this Part of the countrey [sic] Wild Barron and Diserted [sic]. No Agreculter [agriculture] No fire No nothing [but?] Wild Beast [sic] of Every Kind', he wrote; 'and the Papal [people] that Inhabit this Part are uncivilised and savage[,] they gow [go] Naked subsist on Raw flash [flesh] as they kill in the Wild foriest [sic] of this uncultavated [uncultivated] countrie [sic].' It does not seem to have occurred to him that the violent unrest within the region, which

---

63 National Army Museum (NAM) 8303-112-1.

the regiment was there to help subdue, might in some measure account for this state of affairs. There is only the serving soldier's perhaps psychologically necessary detachment. The frontier Africans, as far as he could tell, 'are as the tribes of India', having 'Cheffs' [chiefs] and fighting 'against one another'.[64]

Some 14 or 15 years later he would likely have compared them with the indigenous peoples of Afghanistan. Even as he completed this letter, Witcherley was telling his father that the next communication was likely to come from India, for which the 55th were expected to embark presently. There had clearly been talk of that posting within the regiment already.

The last extant letter from Witcherley to his parents was dated 'Grahams Town 24 October 1828' – that is almost precisely two months after the Battle of Mbholompo. He had, in the meantime, received a letter from his father dated 21 April 1828. Such communications taking months in transit, it arrived at a dramatic moment. 'I Received your letter', Witcherley states, 'when on the Expedition against the wild Zauless [Zulus, as it was believed] and [was] ingaged [sic] the 2nd day after I Received it But [indecipherable word] the almighty god [sic] ordered it that [I] should not be haurt [hurt] So I ascaped [escaped] all Danger.'

If this is so, then the line or lines of communication Colonel Somerset's expedition maintained with Grahamstown were most impressive. Witcherley provides no background to 'the Expedition', but seems to presume some awareness of the Zulus, leaving one to wonder whether he perhaps sent a further letter home in the interim, which has not survived. Instead he described how the 55th inevitably 'suffered sevierly' [severely] from inadequate rations ('one Pound of meat Per day and that such as the Dogs woul[d] not [eat?] at home') and a lack of water, and how the experience 'was no Pleasent [pleasant] thing'. Nonetheless they had, he believed, put an end to what he called 'the hostile enemy' with the loss of only two men '[b]y the Caffers on our Return to the Colony' – a reference not to Mbholompo, but rather the two soldiers murdered by the Xhosa back on the frontier.

Witcherley closed the letter by asking for 'all the particulars' of life at Market Drayton; but he never saw his family and friends again. The 55th Foot finally embarked for Madras in August 1830. A little over a year later, on 2 September 1831, George Witcherley died there 'after a short illness'.[65]

'The Mbolompo Heritage Project'

Nor has the partisanship (if that is the word) surrounding the battle entirely abated. In November 2000 what was called 'The Mbolompo Heritage Project' was officially opened on the approximate site of the battle and MEC

---

64   NAM 8303-112-2.
65   NAM 8303-112-3. Part of the second of these letters was reproduced in the catalogue accompanying the 1999-2001 National Army Museum exhibition *'Ashes and blood'*, wherein the record of Witcherley's death is also quoted: P.B. Boyden, A.J. Guy & M. Harding (eds), *'Ashes and blood': The British Army in South Africa 1795–1914* (London: National Army Museum, 1999), p.200.

(Member of the Executive Council) Nosimo Balindlela gave a speech to mark the occasion. In it she spoke of a memorial 'designed to commemorate our heroes who sacrificed their lives during a very difficult period in our history, namely our people's struggle against oppression and dispossession by the colonialists'. The black people who died on the site lost their lives 'during a particular war of dispossession', and 'In the same way that the blood of these martyrs and heroes nourished the Liberation Struggle, their memory in this public place should serve as a constant reminder … of the present struggle for a better life for all'.[66]

But while few would argue that there was a pressing need to, as the project's aims have it, recognise neglected heritage sites and redress imbalances in the portrayal of the history of the Eastern Cape, this surely was one example where the circumstances, dreadful in their outcome as they were, were not so straightforward. Who was attempting to dispossess whom with Shaka launching his drive south, and Matiwane attacking the Basuto and then the Tambookie/Thembu tribes? In a sense, Balindlela is of course correct. The battle saw the beginning of active colonial involvement in this region. However no historian can be comfortable with the partial presentation of a complex series of events to fit a preconceived position, however well meant and even, in the circumstances, understandable such an impulse may be.

One wonders whether Balindlela's speech was, directly or indirectly, influenced by Julian Cobbing's ill-founded contention that the Fetcani alarm was used by the then acting governor of the Cape, Richard Bourke, as a pretext to 'fetch out' compliant cheap labour (post Ordinance 49) – and that Major Dundas's heterogeneous force and still more Colonel Somerset's body of 55th Foot, Royal Artillery and Cape Mounted Riflemen thus effectively formed the spearhead of a nefarious government enterprise.[67] If so, it derived from a hypothesis that had already been comprehensively debunked by Jeff Peires. Indeed, Peires demonstrated that Dundas was 'a considered advocate of free labour'. Somerset's complicity in the Boers' capture of children to become servants (as frontier Boers had done and, after the Great Trek, would continue to do for decades) was a separate matter.[68]

The Cape Mounted Riflemen, 1828–1834

The Umtata campaign was the greatest extent to which the *mfecane* impinged politically on the colony. In its course British and colonial forces, with the Cape Mounted Rifles as a central component, had been drawn deep into south-east Africa and in their own terms performed well. Thereafter the CMR's attention was for the most part focused again on the colony's

---

66 Speech by MEC Balindlela at the opening of Mbolompo Heritage Project at Lugxogxo village, 11 November 2000 (posted on Eastern Cape Provincial Government website).
67 Cobbing, 'Mfecane as Alibi', pp.501–502.
68 Peires, 'Matiwane's Road to Mbholompo', pp.226–236. It is still more surprising that Stapleton should, in passing, accept Cobbing's discredited thesis, stating that 'in 1828 the Ngwane were targeted by the British army as a possible source of forced labour': *Faku*, p.22. For the Boers' propensity for capturing children in particular, see Liebenberg, *Pretorius*, pp.8, 128, 170–171.

immediate frontier. But Colonel Somerset sought to bring to the attention of his superiors the lasting implications of recent events. Whilst in London in 1833 he submitted an important memoranda on the future defence of the frontier, explaining that the colony's forces had to be capable of meeting dangers originating outside their accustomed sphere of operations, and that it might again become necessary to preserve the frontier chiefs and their populations from the raids of powerful chiefs, such as the new Zulu King, Dingane.

However, as he made clear, the resources at his disposal were hardly equal to such huge responsibilities, for the only permanent feature was 'a small native corps of 200 mounted men which would in reality be barely sufficient for 50 miles of territory'. It would not do to rely over much on summoning Boers; they were understandably reluctant to be taken from their farms, leaving them unproductive and exposed. Therefore, he would be wanting in his duty, Somerset suggested, were he not 'to endeavour to impress on the government the necessity for increasing this most useful Corps to such a strength as may enable it efficiently to protect the frontier'.[69]

The increases he proposed might still be thought modest enough to anyone but a Treasury official: just 150 additional men and 125 horses. But this would, he suggested, 'enable the Commandant to make such a disposition of his forces as would materially tend to prevent the predatory incursions of the Caffers and would give [provide for] a small opposing force to detach to any point in the event of urgent necessity'. It would also 'enable two companies of the Line now detached at the Outposts to be withdrawn and spared for other services'. The additional expense would be offset by removing the need to summon the Boers to undertake commando service so often, during which both they and their horses still had to be fed 'while employed upon their arduous duties', even if they received no pay as such. By being left to work their land these Boers, he argued, would instead 'be able to pay adequate taxes'. (This was a somewhat optimistic view: the frontier Boers, not unlike other settler colonists before them, entertained an increasingly jaundiced view of the tax demands imposed upon them.)

There was also a shortage of seasoned officers, which could not fail but to have a detrimental effect on the regiment's operational efficiency. Colonel Somerset pointed out that 'besides 8 or 10 daily Patrols each requiring to be headed by an officer, there are eight Out Posts of the Corps requiring to have at least two efficient officers for the numerous duties of these Posts'. Taking this into account, it was 'evident that 3 Captains and 6 Subalterns are totally insufficient for those duties'. Matters were worse when one recollected that this left 'no provision for reliefs, sickness or for leave of absence', still less the meeting of emergencies. He compared this with the establishment of the old Cape Corps, which consisted of '4 Troops and 4 Companies'. The frontier was, he asserted, 'never so well protected' as in the years 1824–1827. But 'this efficient Corps, unfortunately for the Frontier, was broken up and a most inadequate Force, in point of numbers, organised in its stead', since when

---

69   Rivett-Carnac, *Hawk's Eye*, p.87.

the colony had had 'no disposable Force' adequate to meet the needs of its security.[70]

The response to this representation and others might not have been immediate, but Colonel Somerset felt he was having some effect and he pressed the newly appointed Governor of the Cape Colony, Sir Benjamin D'Urban, to follow up the matter before he (D'Urban) left London. 'The Horse Guards would, I know, not object', he assured him, 'and Mr Hay [Robert W. Hay, Colonial Under Secretary with responsibility for Africa] seemed impressed with the justice of my observations.' Indeed, he was emboldened to raise the issue of fair pensions for former members of the disbanded Cape Corps. Upon its disbandment a pension of 4½d a day had been awarded to those soldiers discharged. But this was then denied those who had for a time (at government request) continued their service in the Cape Mounted Rifles. Men who had served honourably since the second British occupation of the Cape in 1806 found themselves included in a blindly administered inequitable regulatory prescription. Such an injustice, Colonel Somerset noted, did not 'make recruitment any easier'.[71] However, this period of the regiment's service was to culminate almost immediately in the Sixth Cape Frontier War of 1834–1835.

---

[70] Rivett-Carnac, *Hawk's Eye*, p.87.
[71] Rivett-Carnac, *Hawk's Eye*, p.89.

Bibliography

Amey, G., *City Under Fire: The Bristol Riots and Aftermath* (Guildford: Lutterworth Press, 1979).

Atkinson, C.T. (ed.), *Supplementary Report on the Manuscripts of Robert Graham Esq. of Fintry* (London: HMSO, 1940).

Baldry, W.Y., 'Disbanded Regiments', *Journal of the Society for Army Historical Research*, 14:56, 1935.

Balindlela, Nosimo, speech at the opening of Mbolompo Heritage Project at Lugxogxo village, 11 November 2000. Posted on Eastern Cape Provincial Government website www.ecprov.gov.za/images/pdfFiles/00sport-mbolompo.pdf.

Bannister, S., *Humane Policy; or Justice to the Aborigines of New Settlements, Essential to a Due Expenditure of British Money, and to the Best Interests of the Settlers, with suggestions how to Civilise the Natives by an Improved Administration of Existing Means* (London: Thomas & George Underwood, 1830).

The Border Regiment and The King's Own Royal Border Regiment, Regimental Museum: 55th Foot Digest of Service, unpublished manuscript.

Boyce, William B., *Notes on South African Affairs, From 1834 to 1838; with Reference to the Civil, Political, and Religious Condition of the Colonists and Aborigines* (Graham's Town: Aldum & Harvey, 1838/Cape Town: Struik, facs. reproduction, 1971).

Boyden, P.B., Guy, A.J. & M. Harding (eds) *'Ashes and blood': The British Army in South Africa 1795–1914* (London: National Army Museum, 1999).

Butler, L., *The Annals of the King's Royal Rifle Corps: Volume I, 'The Royal Americans'* (London: Smith, Elder & Co., 1913).

Campbell, C.T., *British South Africa: A History of the Colony of the Cape of Good Hope from its Conquest 1795 to the Settlement of Albany by the British Emigration of 1819, with notices of some of the British Settlers of 1820* (London & Cape Town: John Haddon & Co., 1897).

Chartrand, R., *Émigré and Foreign Troops in British Service (2) 1803–15* (Oxford: Osprey, 2000).

Cobbing, J., 'The Mfecane as Alibi: Thoughts on Dithakong and Mbolompo', *Journal of African History*, 29, 1988.

Cobley, A., 'Sarah Ann Gill's Pastor: Hero or Villain? The Reverend William Shrewsbury in Barbados and South Africa', paper delivered as the Fifth Annual Sarah Ann Gill Memorial Lecture, at the Frank Collymore Hall, Bridgetown, Barbados, 11 May 2011, ResearchGate.net/publication/313302119.

Crooks, Major J., *Historical Records of the Royal African Corps* (Dublin: Browne & Nolan, 1925).

Cory, G.E., *The Rise of South Africa: A History of the Origin of South African Colonisation and of its Development Towards the East from the Earliest Times to 1857: vol. I, From the Earliest Times to the Year 1820* (London: Longmans, Green & Co., 1910).

Cory, G.E., *The Rise of South Africa: vol. II, From 1820 to 1834* (London: Longmans, Green & Co., 1913).
Cory, G.E., *The Rise of South Africa: vol. III, From 1834 to 1840* (London: Longmans, Green & Co., 1919).
Couzens, T., *Battles of South Africa* (Claremont, South Africa: David Philip, 2004).
De Villiers, J., *Die Cape Regiment, 1806–1817, 'n Koloniale Regiment in Britse Diens* (Pretoria: Archives Year Book, Die Staatsdrukker, 1989).
De Villiers, J., 'Perspective on John Graham and the Fourth Cape Eastern Frontier War', *New Contree*, 68, December 2013.
Dictionary of South African Biography (DSAB) 5 vols (Cape Town & Pretoria: Human Sciences Research Council, 1968–1987).
Dracopoli, J.L., *Sir Andries Stockenström 1792–1864: The Origins of the Racial Conflict in South Africa* (Cape Town: A.A. Balkema, 1969).
Duffill, M.. *Mungo Park* (Edinburgh: NMS Publishing, 1999).
Ellenberger, D.F., *History of the Basuto Ancient and Modern, Compiled by D. Fred. Ellenberger, V.D.M. and written in English by J.C. Macgregor, Assistant Commissioner, under the auspices of the Basutoland Government* (London: Caxton Publishing Company, 1912).
Elphick, R. & H. Giliomee (eds), *The Shaping of South African Society, 1652–1840* (Cape Town: Maskew Miller Longman, 1989).
Etherington, N., *The Great Treks: The Transformation of Southern Africa, 1815–1854* (London: Longman, 2001).
Fast, H.H. (ed.), *The Journal and Selected Letters of Rev. William J. Shrewsbury 1826–1835, First Missionary to the Transkei* (Johannesburg: The Graham's Town Series, Witwatersrand University Press, 1994).
Freer, Major W.J., *The Thirty-Eighth Regiment of Foot, Now The First Battalion of the South Staffordshire Regiment* (London: Harrison & Sons, 1916).
Fuller, J.F.C., *British Light Infantry in the Eighteenth Century* (London: Hutchinson, 1925).
Gledhill, E. & J. Gledhill, *In the Steps of Piet Retief* (Cape Town: Human & Rousseau, 1980).
Hamilton, C. (ed.), *The Mfecane Aftermath: Reconstructive Debates in Southern African History* (Johannesburg & Pietermaritzburg: Witwatersrand University Press/ University of Natal Press, 1995).
Harington, A.L., *The Graham's Town Journal and The Great Trek, 1834–1843* (Johannesburg: Archives Year Book, Die Staatsdrukker, 1973).
Haythornthwaite, P.J., *The Armies of Wellington* (London: Brockhampton Press, 1998).
Holmes, R., *Redcoat: The British Soldier in the Age of Horse and Musket* (London: HarperCollins, 2001).
Holt, B., *Greatheart of the Border: A Life of John Brownlee, Pioneer Missionary in South Africa* (King William's Town: The South African Missionary Museum, 1976).
Hutton, C.W. (ed.), *The Autobiography of the late Sir Andries Stockenström, Bart., Sometime Lieutenant-Governor of the Eastern Province of the Colony of the Cape of Good Hope*, vol. I (Cape Town: J.C. Juta & Co., 1887/Cape Town: Struik, facs. reproduction, 1964).
Kay, S., *Travels and Researches in Caffraria: Describing the Character, Customs, and Moral Condition of the Tribes inhabiting that Portion of Southern Africa: with Historical and Topographical Remarks Illustrative of the State and Prospects of the British Settlement in its Borders, and the Introduction of Christianity, and the Progress of Civilization* (London: John Mason, 1833).
Keppel-Jones, A. (ed.), *Philipps, 1820 Settler: His Letters* (Pietermaritzburg: Shuter & Shooter, 1960).
King, H., *Richard Bourke* (Melbourne: Oxford University Press, 1971).
Laband, J., *The Assassination of King Shaka* (Johannesburg: Jonathan Ball, 2017).

Laband, J., *The Land Wars: The Dispossession of the Khoisan and AmaXhosa in the Cape Colony* (Cape Town: Penguin, Random House, 2020).

Lambert, D. & A. Lester, 'Missionary politics and the captive audience: William Shrewsbury in the Caribbean and the Cape Colony', in Lambert, D. and A. Lester (eds), *Colonial Lives Across the British Empire: Imperial Careering in the Long Nineteenth Century* (Cambridge: Cambridge University Press, 2006).

Le Cordeur, B.A. (ed.), *The Journal of Charles Lennox Stretch* (Grahamstown: The Graham's Town Series, Maskew Miller Longman for Rhodes University, 1988).

Liebenberg, B.J., *Andries Pretorius, Voortrekker Leader in Natal: Blood River to Congella, 1838-1842*, translated and revised by H. Driver (London: Barksdale Books, 2020).

Liddell Hart, B.H., *Thoughts on War* (London: Faber & Faber, 1944/repr. Staplehurst: Spellmount, 1999).

Longford, E., *Wellington: The Years of the Sword* (London: Weidenfeld & Nicolson, 1969).

Low, C.R., *Soldiers of the Victorian Age*, vol. I (London: Chapman & Hall, 1880).

Maclennan, B., *A Proper Degree of Terror: John Graham and the Cape's Eastern Frontier* (Johannesburg: Ravan Press, 1986).

Millar, A.K., *Plantagenet in South Africa: Lord Charles Somerset* (Cape Town: Oxford University Press, 1965).

Milton, J., *The Edges of War: A History of Frontier Wars (1702–1878)* (Cape Town: Juta & Co., 1983).

Mitford-Barberton, I., *Comdt. Holden Bowker: An 1820 Settler book including unpublished records of the Frontier Wars* (Cape Town & Pretoria: Human & Rousseau, 1970).

Moodie, D.C.F., *The History of the Battles and Adventures of the British, The Boers, and the Zulus, etc., in Southern Africa from the Time of Pharaoh Necho to 1880, with Copious Chronology*, vol. I. (Cape Town: Murray & St. Leger, 1888/London: Frank Cass & Co., Library of African Studies, facs. reproduction, 1968).

Moloja (as recounted to J.M. Orpen), 'The Story of the "Fetcani Horde" by One of Themselves', *Cape Quarterly Review*, 1, 2, 1881–1882.

Mostert, N., *Frontiers: The Epic of South Africa's Creation and the Tragedy of the Xhosa People* (New York: Alfred A. Knopf, 1992).

National Army Museum (NAM) 8303-112-1, Private George Witcherley, 55th Foot, to his parents, Cape Town, Jun. 182? (date indecipherable).

NAM 8303-112-2, Private George Witcherley, 55th Foot, to his parents, Grahamstown, 14 Jan. 1828.

NAM 8303-112-3, Private George Witcherley, 55th Foot, to his parents, Grahamstown, 24 Oct. 1828.

Noakes, G., *A Historical Account of the Services of the 34th & 55th Regiments, The Linked Line Battalions in the 2nd or Cumberland & Westmorland Sub-District Brigade, from the Periods of their Formation until the Present Time* (Carlisle: Thurnam & Sons, 1875).

Orpen, J.M., *The Story of the 'Fetcani Horde' by One of Themselves: Moloja, of Jozani's village, at Masite, near Morija, Basutoland* (Cape Town: 1882).

Peires, J.B., *The House of Phalo: A History of the Xhosa People in the Days of Their Independence* (Berkeley & Los Angeles: University of California Press, 1982).

Peires, J.B., *The Dead Will Arise: Nongqawuse and the Great Xhosa Cattle-Killing Movement of 1856–7* (Bloomington: Indiana University Press, 1989).

Peires, J.B., 'The British and the Cape, 1814–1834', in Elphick, R. and Giliomee, H. (eds), *The Shaping of South African Society, 1652–1840* (Cape Town: Maskew Miller Longman, 1989).

Peires, J.B., 'Matiwane's Road to Mbholompo: A Reprieve for the Mfecane?' in Hamilton, C. (ed.), *The Mfecane Aftermath: Reconstructive Debates in Southern African History* (Johannesburg & Pietermaritzburg: Witwatersrand University Press/University of Natal Press, 1995).

BIBLIOGRAPHY

Pretorius, J. Celestine, 'Robert H. Dingley: Amateurkunstenaar van die Oosgrens (1813-1818)', *Historia* 37(2), November 1992.

Pringle, T., *Narrative of a Residence in South Africa, with introduction, biographical and historical notes by A.M. Lewin Robinson, B.A., Ph.D., F.L.A.* (Cape Town: Struik, 1966).

Rivett-Carnac, D.E., *Hawk's Eye: Lieutenant-General Sir Henry Somerset K.C.B., K.H.* (Cape Town: Howard Timmins, 1966).

Sadler, C. (ed.), *Never a Young Man: Extracts from the Letters and Journals of the Rev. William Shaw* (Cape Town: HAUM, 1967).

Sanders, P., *Moshoeshoe, Chief of the Sotho* (London: Heinemann, 1975).

Shrewsbury, Rev. W. J., *Correspondence 1827–1828*, in Wesleyan Methodist Missionary Society South Africa Correspondence, MMS Box 301, Special Collections, School of Oriental & African Studies, University of London.

Smithers, A.J., *The Kaffir Wars 1779–1877: 19th Century Military Campaigns* (London: Leo Cooper, 1973).

Stapleton, T.J., *Faku: Rulership and Colonialism in the Mpondo Kingdom (c. 1760–1867)* (Waterloo, Ontario: Wilfrid Laurier University Press, 2001).

Steenkamp, W., *Assegais, Drums and Dragoons: A Military and Social History of the Cape 1510–1806* (Johannesburg & Cape Town: Jonathan Ball, 2012).

Storey, W.K., *Guns, Race, and Power in Colonial South Africa* (Cambridge: African Studies Series, Cambridge University Press, 2011).

Streak, M., *The Afrikaner as Viewed by the English 1795–1854* (Cape Town: Struik, 1974).

Tylden, Major G., *The Armed Forces of South Africa* (Johannesburg: Trophy Press, 1982).

Van Warmelo, N.J. (ed.), *History of Matiwane and the amaNgwane Tribe as told by Msebenzi to his kinsman Albert Hlongwane, edited and supplemented by Archive Documents and other material by N.J. van Warmelo, Government Ethnologist* (Pretoria: Department of Native Affairs, 1938).

Walker, E.A. (ed.), *The Cambridge History of the British Empire, vol. VIII: South Africa, Rhodesia and the High Commission Territories* (Cambridge: Cambridge University Press, second edition, 1963).

Wallis, J.P.R. (ed.), *The Matabele Journals of Robert Moffat, 1829–1860*, vol. I (London: Chatto & Windus, 1945).

Wells, J.C., *The Return of Makhanda: Exploring the Legend* (Scottsville, Pietermaritzburg: University of KwaZulu-Natal Press, 2012).

Young, P.J., *Boot and Saddle: A Narrative Record of the Cape Regiment, the British Cape Mounted Riflemen, the Frontier Armed Mounted Police, and the Colonial Cape Mounted Riflemen* (Cape Town: Maskew Miller, 1955).

Index

Abbey, Major (72nd Foot), 69
Addo Forest, 19
Aitchison, Captain Robert Scott, 111–12
Aitchison, Lieutenant, 61
Albany (district), 82, 84, 92, 94, 99, 101–4, 108, 114
Alexander, du Pre, 2nd Earl of Caledon, 16–17, 83
Alexander, Henry, 21, 83
Alacrity (transport ship) 53, 55
Algoa Bay, 18, 23, 53, 55, 108–9
Amalinde, Battle of (1818), 46–50, 58, 64–65, 100
Amasizi/amaZizi *see* Zizi
Andrews, Major, 91–92
Arbuthnot, Colonel Thomas (later General: Deputy QMG, Cape Colony, 1810–1812), 27

Bailie, Charles Theodore (1820 Settler), 99–100
Baird, General Sir David, 15, 43
Balindlela, MEC Nosimo, 121
Bannister, Saxe (lawyer and humanitarian campaigner), 115, 116fn,
Barrow, John (private secretary to Lord Macartney, Governor of the Cape 1796–1802: his *Account of Travels into the Interior of Southern Africa* published in various vols between 1801–1806), 18, 21
Bashee River, 79, 99, 101–2, 110, 111fn
Batavian regime (1803–1806), 13, 13fn, 15, 37
Bathurst, Henry, 3rd Earl, 41–42, 51, 82–83, 87–88
Bathurst (settlement), 61fn, 84, 100–1
Basuto *see* Sotho
Bawana *see* Powana
Begha River, 85, 85fn

Bell, Colonel John (Secretary, Cape Government), 104
Bethelsdorp (LMS mission station), 57
Bhaca (northern Nguni peoples/tribe), 91
Bhurhu (Xhosa chief, Hintsa's brother), 76, 78–80
Biddulph, W. (1820 Settler), 100
Bird, Colonel Christopher Chapman (Secretary, Cape Government), 71fn, 76, 78–80
Blaauwberg, Battle of (1806), 15
Black Kei River, 90
'Blundering Commando' (1818), 45–46, 51, 63
Boers: background, 13; fear being conscripted into British Army, 18; Colonel Graham's inconsistent view of, 18, 20; commandos, 17, 19–21, 31, 52, 56, 69, 71, 79–80, 92, 96, 103, 114, 122; propensity for capturing native children, 112, 114, 121, 121fn; no substitute for a permanent mounted force, 88, 122
Boesak, Jan (Khoi hunter/convert), 66
Botha's Hill, 58, 60
Bourke, General Richard, 88, 93–94, 96, 111fn, 112fn, 113, 113fn, 114fn, 121
Bowker, Bertram Egerton (1820 Settler), 100–4, 105fn, 106fn, 107
Bowker, John Mitford (1820 Settler), 100–2
Bowker, Thomas Holden (1820 Settler), 100–1, 101fn, 102
Bowker, William Monkhouse (1820 Settler), 100–2
Boyce, William Binnington (WMS missionary), 113fn, 116–17, 117fn
Brereton, Colonel Thomas, 50–56, 58, 63, 74

INDEX

British Army, colonial: Cape Regiment, 15–16, 16fn, 17, 17fn, 18–19, 21, 24–28, 30–31, 34, 43, 43fn, 45, 51–54, 57, 57fn, 60, 88, 108fn; Cape Corps of Infantry and Cavalry (Cape Light Infantry and Cape Cavalry), 43, 45, 52–53, 56, 58–59, 61, 66–69, 86–90, 93, 111, 122–23; Cape Mounted Rifles/Riflemen, 89, 93, 108, 108fn, 109–10, 121, 123 (*see also* desertions)

British Army, regular: 20th Foot, 60; 21st Light Dragoons, 16–17, 17fn, 22, 25, 27, 30, 42, 93; 38th Foot, 52–53, 55, 58, 61, 63–64, 69, 84; 54th Foot, 69; 55th Foot, 108, 109fn, 114, 118–21; 60th Foot, 20, 22–25, 30–32, 38, 40, 42, 80; 72nd Foot, 53, 61, 69, 84–85; 83rd Foot, 17, 17fn, 23–25, 30, 42; 93rd Foot, 16–17, 17fn; Royal African Corps, 23, 38–40, 45, 49–50, 58, 68, 84; Royal Artillery, 17, 17fn, 19, 56, 108, 121; Royal Engineers, 69 (*see also* desertions)

Brock, Major (55th Foot), 108
Brownlee, John (missionary), 56, 57fn, 90
Bruinjes Hoegte, 21
Buffalo River, 72, 75, 79
Bushmen *see* San
Butterworth (WMS mission station), 65, 94, 96–97, 99, 101, 109–10, 116

Caledon Code, 33
Caledon, 2nd Earl *see* Alexander, du Pre
Caledon River, 91, 106
Campbell, A.G. ('Justus'), 25
Campbell, Captain Duncan (Civil Commissioner, Albany and Somerset), 94, 114
Campbell, Colin Turing, 68, 68fn
Cape Malays, 26
Cape Corps of Infantry and Cavalry *see* British Army
Cape Mounted Rifles/Riflemen *see* British Army
Cape Regiment *see* British Army
Cape Town, 15–17, 30, 34, 38, 45, 53, 55, 63, 69, 76, 80, 81, 85, 92–93, 95, 108, 119
Cartwright, Lieutenant, 61
Cawood, Jas/James (1820 Settler), 100
Cawood, John (1820 Settler), 100
ceded territory, the, 81–82, 84
Chumie/Tyhume (Glasgow Missionary Society station), 107
Chumie/Tyhume/Tyumie River, 28, 46, 70, 92

Chungwa (Gqunukhwebe Xhosa chief), 19–20, 47, 75
Cloete, Captain (later General) Abraham Josias, 17, 96
Cobbing, Julian, 105fn, 121, 121fn
Cockcroft, Mark (1820 Settler), 100
Collins, Colonel Richard, 51, 82
Corps Bastaard Hottentots, 15
Corps van Pandoeren, 15
Corps Vrye Hottentotten, 15
Cory, George, 33, 61, 62, 68, 85, 105fn, 110, 114
Cox, Major (later Colonel) William, 89
Cradock, Sir John Francis, 17, 18fn, 20, 20fn, 21, 26, 29–32, 34, 83
Cuyler, Colonel Jacob, 19, 31, 36, 54, 72

Debe Nek, 46–47, 100
De Bruin's Drift, 53
desertions, 19, 38, 40–44, 49, 51, 61, 70, 73, 78–79
De Villiers, Johan, 19, 43
Dingane kaSenzangakhona (Shaka's half-brother and successor), 106–7, 115, 122
Donkin, Sir Rufane, 82, 84–85, 87
Dundas Commando, 93, 99
Dundas, Major (later General) William Bolden (*Landdrost*, Albany District/Civil Commissioner, Albany and Somerset), 92, 94, 96, 99, 101, 101fn, 102, 103, 103fn, 104–5, 105fn, 106–7, 109, 117, 121
Durandt, Commandant, 108, 114
D'Urban, Sir Benjamin, 123
Dutch East India Company, 13, 15

Elizabeth and Susan (schooner), 93
Evatt, Captain Francis (21st Light Dragoons, Government Resident, Port Elizabeth), 93, 96+

Faku (paramount chief/king of the Mpondo), 96–97, 97fn, 99, 102, 113fn, 116–17
Farewell, Lieutenant Francis George (Port Natal trader/settler), 93
'Fetcani' alarm, 48, 87, 99, 109, 121
Fifth Frontier War (1818–1819), 38–86
Fingoes *see* Mfengu
first British occupation (1795–1803), 13, 15
Fish River, 13–14, 17, 19–20, 24, 28, 30–31, 33–34, 36, 43, 45, 55–56, 58–59, 69–73, 82–86, 101
Fobo (Thembu sub-chief), 103

129

Fort Beaufort, 96, 107, 109
Fort Willshire, 81, 84
Fourth Frontier War (1811–1812), 14, 16–26, 47, 51, 83, 93
Foxcroft, Thomas (1820 Settler), 100
Fransche Hoek Pass, 85
Fraser, Colonel George Sackville, 19, 28, 36, 39, 43, 45–46, 51, 53, 54–55, 58, 58fn, 59fn, 60, 60fn, 63, 64, 65fn, 67, 67fn, 68, 68fn, 69–70, 72, 75, 82
Fraser, Colonel John, 38, 44
Fredericksburg (settlement), 85–86
Frend, Captain (55th Foot), 108
Funa's Kraal, 70
Fynn, Henry Francis (Port Natal trader/settler), 94–95, 102

Galela *see* Mtyelela
Gcaleka (Xhosa peoples/tribe), 14, 46–47, 49, 81, 97, 114, 116, 118
Gcina/amaGcina (Thembu clan), 91
Gethin, Captain (72nd Foot), 53
Gordon, General Sir James Willoughby, 44–45
Goree, 38–40, 50
Gqunukhwebe (Xhosa peoples/tribe), 19, 47–48, 75
Graaff-Reinet, 13, 19, 26–27, 31, 36, 51–52, 70, 75, 90, 108
Graham, Colonel John: command of Cape Regiment, 17, 17fn,; tensions with frontier Boers, 17–19, 21; Fourth Frontier War, 14–15, 18, 18fn, 19, 19fn, 20, 20fn, 22, 24, 24fn, 25; pejorative view of Xhosa, 20–21, 24; founding of Grahamstown, 26–30; response to call for troop reductions, 30–31; 'Instructions to Commanders of Posts', 31–34; love of Cape Regiment and Khoikhoi generally, 21, 26; Commandant of Simon's Town, 40, 68; critical of Willshire's defence of Grahamstown, 68–69
Graham, General Sir Thomas (Lord Lynedoch), 34
Grahamstown, 26, 28–31, 33, 35–36, 45, 50–53, 57, 69–70, 74, 82, 84–85, 91, 94, 108–9, 119–20; foundation of, 26–30; Battle of (1819), 48–49, 58–69, 76, 79
Gretta (Xhosa chief), 45–46
Greyling, Jan Christiaan, 19
Grosvenor (shipwreck), 97
Gurwood, Colonel John, 44

Habana (Xhosa chief), 45–46

Hanglip Mountains, 92
Harding, Captain William, 60, 67
Hart, Lieutenant Robert, 25, 27–28
Hawana (Ngwane chief, brother of Matiwane), 106
Hay, Robert William (Colonial Under-Secretary) 123
Helicon, HMS, 96
Hintsa (Chief of the Gcaleka people and Xhosa paramount chief), 14, 26, 46–50, 58, 65, 75–76, 78–81, 94–95, 97, 99–103, 109–10, 114
Holloway, Major William (RE), 69–70
Hottentot (demoded usage) *see* Khoikhoi
Hottentot Ligte Infanterie, 1598761uiop[9op0[
Hlubi (northern Nguni peoples/tribe), 106, 115
Hunt, Ensign (RAC), 53
Huntly, Captain, 68

Isaacs, Nathaniel (Port Natal trader/settler), 93
imiDange (Xhosa peoples/tribe) 19
Intaba-ka-Ndoda *see* Ntaba kaNdoda

'Justus' *see* A.G. Campbell
Jingqi/amaJingqi (Xhosa peoples/tribe), 50

Kabousie River, 76, 79
kaffir, origin of pejorative term, (demoded usage) *see* Xhosa
Kaffir/Kaffirs Drift, 53, 58, 69, 101
Kat River, 28, 35, 37, 46, 52, 57, 70, 92, 96
Kat River Conference (1817), 35–37
Kay, Stephen (WMS missionary), 111fn, 115, 116, 116fn, 117–118
Kei River, 72, 75–77, 79, 90, 92, 94, 99, 101, 109
Keiskamma River, 28, 51, 54–55, 70, 72, 74–75, 79–82, 84–85, 92, 100
Khoikhoi (contemporary term was 'Hottentot', use of which is demoded), 15–16, 21, 26–27, 33, 51, 54, 56, 59, 66, 68–69, 90fn, 101, 110
King, James Saunders (Port Natal trader/settler), 93–94, 96
Klaas Smits River, 90
Kobe (Xhosa chief, son of Chungwa), 75
Komgha, 101
kwaMatiwane (Matiwane's place of execution at uMgunundlovu), 115

Ladybrand, 99, 106–7, 115

INDEX

Langalibalele (Hlubi chief), 115
Linde, Commandant Jacobus, 70
Lochenberg, Nicholas (Boer living among Gcaleka Xhosa), 51, 95
Lombard, *Hemraad* Christoffel, 21
Lombard's Post, 82
London Missionary Society (LMS), 35, 57
Lovedale (GMS mission station), 107
Lugxogxo (modern-day village/settlement), 111, 121fn
Lyster, Major Thomas, 43

MacCarthy, Charles, 44
Macdonald, Private, 53
Mackay, William Macdonald (Landdrost, Somerset East), 91–92, 106
Madikane (*Bhaca* chief), 91
Makanna *see* Nxele
Maketa ('boy king' of the 'Masootoo'), 91–92
Mambookies *see* Mpondo
Mantatees/Mantatese *see* Tlokwa
Manxoyi (Xhosa chief, reputedly Ngqika's commander at Amalinde), 49
Maqoma (Xhosa chief, son of Ngqika), 49–50, 70, 82, 92, 100
Masootoo (Cape Corps identified Transorange tribe), 92
Matabele (Ndebele peoples), 106, 113
'Matuana Mountain', 111
Matiwane (chief of the Ngwane), 92, 106, 107, 111, 113, 114, 115, 115fn, 121,
Mbolompo, Battle of (1828), 100 (map)
Mbolompo Heritage Project, 120–21, 121fn
Mbozamboza (Zulu *induna*, aide to Sothobe kaMpangalala), 94, 96
McNeil, Captain Donald, 27–28
Mdalidephu (Xhosa deity), 58, 64
Mdepa (Tshomane chief), 97
Mdushane (Xhosa chief, son of Ndlambe), 47, 47fn, 49, 58
Meyer, Lucas, 27–29
Mfecane, the *see also* Fetcani and Mfengu, 91, 91fn, 105fn, 121fn
Mfengu, the (hungry/wandering peoples), 94
Mill, Colonel (55th Foot), 108, 114
Milton, Regimental Surgeon W.W., 28–29
Mnyaluza (Xhosa chief), 76
Moffat, Robert (LMS missionary), 113, 113fn
Moloja (Ngwane warrior),
Moodie, Benjamin (pioneer coloniser), 83, 86

Moodie, Donald, 86
Moodie, John Wedderburn Dunbar, 86
Morley (WMS mission station), 97
Moshoeshoe (sometimes spelt Moshweshwe: founder and first paramount chief of the southern Sotho/BaSotho), 91, 106, 106fn, 115
Mostert, Noel, 55, 73fn, 82fn
Mount Coke (WMS mission station), 101
Mpondo (Xhosa-speaking peoples/tribe domiciled between the Mtata and Mzimkhulu rivers), 90fn, 93, 97–99, 101–2, 113fn, 117
Mpondoland, 95–96
Mtyelela (chief, Thembu amaGcina clan), 91–92
Mzilikazi kaMashobana (leader of the Matabele), 113
Mzimkhulu River (eastern boundary of Mpondo kingdom), 102

Napier, Sir George, 44, 117
Natal, 51, 90fn, 92, 96, 106, 117
Natawana (reputed Zulu chief), 102
Ndlambe (Xhosa chief, regent of the amaRharhabe and uncle of Ngqika), 14–15, 35–37, 45–47, 49–53, 55–56, 68, 70, 73, 75–76, 78–80, 85
Ndlambe/ama-Ndlambe (Xhosa peoples/tribe), 46, 49–51, 53–54, 56, 58, 60, 70–73, 76
Nel, Louis, 21
Ngqakayi River, 81
Ngqika (Chief of the amaRharhabe or western Xhosa), 14–15, 35–37, 42, 45–50, 50fn, 52–53, 57–58, 61, 63, 70, 73–74, 76, 78–2, 84, 107
Ngqungqushe (father of Faku), 97
Ngubengcuka (known to Europeans as Vusani: Thembu paramount), 90, 97, 99, 102–4, 105fn, 107, 110, 113fn, 114
Nguni-speaking peoples (broadly, southern Nguni refers to IsiXhosa and northern Nguni to IsiZulu), 90–91
Ngwane/amaNgwane (Zulu-speaking peoples/tribe), 92–92, 99, 105fn, 106–7, 111, 113, 115–17, 121fn
Nquka, Hendrik (Ngqika's interpreter, Xhosa spy), 58, 61, 68
Nortjie, Field Cornet, 20
Ntaba kaNdoda, 46–47

Ordinance 49, 121
Orange River, 13, 51, 91
Orpen, Joseph Millerd, 107

131

Owen Glendower (frigate), 108

Park, Mungo, 39, 39fn
passes, issuing of, 33, 36
'Patross, John' (Xhosa Christian covert, survivor of battles of Amalinde and Grahamstown), 65
Peacock, Sergeant, 53
Peddie (modern-day settlement, site of Ndlambe's Great Place), 45, 85
Peires, J.B., 82, 106–7, 107fn, 112fn, 114, 121,
Phatho (Xhosa chief, son of Chungwa), 47–48, 48fn, 49
Philipps, Thomas (1820 Settler), 35, 95, 95fn, 104, 104fn
Phillips, J. (British settler), 100
Phillips, Edward (British settler), 100
Port Beaufort, 35
Port Elizabeth, 93–94, 96, 108
Port Natal, 17, 93, 96, 100
Pretorius, Andries Wilhelmus Jacobus (Voortrekker leader), 90fn, 115, 115fn, 117fn, 121fn
Pringle, Thomas, 25, 60, 64, 64fn, 66, 67, 67fn, 73, 73fn, 74

reprisal system *see* spoor law
Reynell, Colonel Thomas (Military Secretary to Sir John Cradock), 20fn, 21, 21fn, 24fn, 25fn, 30, 30fn, 31fn, 34fn
Rharhabe/amaRharhabe (Xhosa peoples/western Xhosa), 14–15, 45–47, 48fn, 49–50, 70
Retief, Piet (Voortrekker leader), 19, 33fn, 35, 62, 115
Robben Island, 42, 81, 108
Rogers, Major George, 40–41, 54
Ross, Lieutenant, 107
Royal African Corps *see* British Army

Salt, Elizabeth (née Covare), 66
San (Bushmen, hunter-gatherer peoples), 13, 90fn
Scott, Colonel Maurice (Commandant of the Frontier), 87
second British occupation (1806–), 13, 126
Settlers (1820), 35, 68, 68fn, 84, 104, 116fn,
Shaka kaSenzangakhona (creator of the Zulu kingdom), 64, 64fn, 92–97, 99, 101–2, 105–6, 111, 114–15, 118, 121

Shaw, Rev. William (Director, Wesleyan Methodist Missionary Society in South Africa), 48–49, 65, 95, 95fn, 96–67, 101
Shepstone, John William (1820 Settler/WMS missionary), 97
Shrewsbury, Rev. William James (WMS missionary), 47, 48, 48fn, 49, 49fn, 50, 65, 65fn, 94–95, 96–97, 99, 101, 103fn, 109, 110, 118–19
Simon's Town, 34, 40, 68
Skerrett, Colonel (55th Foot), 108
Slagter's Nek, 33, 42
Smit, Commandant Abram, 75
Smith, Captain Thomas Charlton, 117
Somerset (frontier district), 94, 114
Somerset East, 25, 91
Somerset, Lord Charles Henry, 17, 34–37, 40, 42–46, 50–56, 80–84, 87; interest in Cape Corps even to uniforms and weapons issued, 87; sees need of mounted element, 42, 87–88; on suitability of Khoikhoi for frontier/bush warfare, 87–88; sanctions enrolment of Mantatees/Mantatese refugees as apprentices to non-slave holders, 90
Somerset, Colonel (later General) Henry, 87–93, 96, 99, 105fn, 107–12, 112fn, 113, 115, 117–18, 120–23
Somerset, General Fitzroy James Henry (later Field Marshal Lord Raglan), 44, 118
Sotho/Sesotho (specifically the southern Sotho/BaSotho peoples under Moshoeshoe),
Sothobe kaMpangalala (Zulu *induna*), 91, 93, 106–7
spoor law, 36
Steenkamp, Johannes Harmen (Field Cornet, Tarka District), 90–92
Stephanos (Xhosa spy), 63
Stockenström, Anders (1757–1811), 19, 19fn, 26
Stockenström, Andries (1792–1864), 27–28, 36, 43, 51–52, 67, 70–71, 72–73, 73fn, 74, 75–76, 78–80, 117, 18
Stormberg, the, 90, 92
Stormberg Spruit, 91
Storey, Major (Royal Artillery), 108, 113
Stretch, Charles Lennox (soldier, native commissioner and politician, known as 'the philanthropic commissioner': in 1819 an ensign in the 38th Foot), 55, 58fn
Sumbley, Captain (55th Foot), 119

INDEX

Sunday's River, 19

Tambookies *see* Thembu
Tayi, son of Mdalidephu (Xhosa deity), 64
Thaba Bosiu (Moshoeshoe's mountain stronghold), 106
Thembu (autonomous Xhosa-speaking people located to the north of Gcaleka Xhosa), 76, 79, 90–92, 97–99, 101–4, 105, 105fn, 106–7, 110, 113fn, 114, 116, 118, 121
Theopolis (mission station), 66
Thuthula (Xhosa concubine), 14
Tlokwa (also known as Mantatees/Mantatese: Sotho-speaking peoples/tribe), 106, 115
Trappes, Captain Charles, 60–61, 66
Trekboers, 13, 26
Trompetter's Drift (Fish River), 28, 45, 58, 71–72, 105
Tshomane (peoples/tribe: autonomous Mpondo chiefdom),
Tyumie/Tyhume River *see* Chumie
Twecu River, 47

Uitenhage, 19, 31, 33–34, 36–37, 54, 57, 69, 72, 93, 108
Upper Kaffir Drift, 53, 69
uHlanga (Xhosa deity/creator), 57
Umtata (now Mthatha, present-day town), 93, 97, 99, 101, 101fn, 105, 107, 111, 121
Umtata River, 103–4, 107, 111, 117–18
Umzimvubu River, 94
uShiyi (Ngwane regiment), 107

Van der Kemp, Dr. Johannes Theodorus (LMS missionary), 26, 57
Van der Lingen, Aart Antonij (Chaplain, Cape Regiment), 26, 57, 57fn
Van de Merve (burgher), 21

Van der Riet (*Landdrost*, Port Elizabeth), 93, 96
Van der Walt, Tjaart (Field Cornet), 76
Van Wyk, Stephanus (Field Cornet/Commandant), 76, 108, 114
Vusani *see* Ngubengcuka: Thembu paramount

Wesleyan Methodist Missionary Society (WMS), 48, 65fn, 94, 111, 115–17
Wesleyville (WMS mission station), 487–48, 57, 101
Whetham, General Arthur, 23
White Kei River, 90
White Mfolozi River (Natal), 106
Whittiker, Private James (55th Foot), 119
William Van Aardt's Ford (Fish River), 33
Williams, Joseph (LMS missionary), 35, 46, 57
Willshire, Colonel (later General) Thomas, 49, 54–56, 58–61, 63–64, 66–70, 70fn, 71–76, 78–82, 84
Winterberg, 50, 99
Witcherley, Private George (55th Foot), 118–20, 120fn
Witsi (Tlokwa/Mantatese chief), 115
Woolridge (modern-day settlement), 85

Xasa (Xhosa chief), 45, 46
Xhosa *see under particular chiefs/peoples*, 13–15, 17, 19–22, 26, 30–37, 41–43, 45–53, 55–61, 63–73, 73fn, 75–77, 79–82, 84, 86, 90, 90fn, 91–93, 94–95, 97, 99, 1405, 114, 117, 120

Zikhali (Ngwane chief, son of Matiwane), 115
Zizi (Amasizi/amaZizi: peoples/tribe), 106
Zuurveld, 13, 15, 30–31, 41, 43, 46, 51, 70, 83, 86
Zulu, 68fn, 73, 90, 92–97, 99, 102–106, 106fn, 107, 109–11, 115, 120, 122